**TEACHER'S PET PUBLICATIONS**

PUZZLE PACK
for
That Was Then, This Is Now

based on the book by
S. E. Hinton

Written by
Mary B. Collins

© 2005 Teacher's Pet Publications
All Rights Reserved

The materials in this packet are copyrighted
by Teacher's Pet Publications, Inc.

These pages may be duplicated by the purchaser
for use in the purchaser's own classroom.

Copying any of these materials and distributing them
for any other purpose is a violation of the copyright laws.

© 2005 Teacher's Pet Publications, Inc.
www.tpet.com

INTRODUCTION

If you already own the LitPlan for this title, this Puzzle Pack will refresh your Unit Resource Materials and Vocabulary Resource Materials sections plus give you additional materials you can substitute into the tests. If you do not already have a complete LitPlan, these pages will give you some supplemental materials to use with your own plan. There are two main groups of materials: one set for unit words (such as characters' names, symbols, places, etc.) and one set for vocabulary words associated with the book.

WORD LIST

There is a word list for both the unit words and the vocabulary words. These lists show you which words are being used in the materials and the clues or definitions being used for those words. You may want to give students a word list with clues/definitions to help them, or you may want students to only have a word list (without clues/definitions) if you want them to work a little harder. Both are available for duplication. The word lists can also be your "calling key" for the bingo games.

FILL IN THE BLANK AND MATCHING

There are 4 each of the fill in the blank and matching worksheets for both the unit and vocabulary words. These pages can be used either as extra worksheets for students or as objective parts of a unit test. They can be done individually if students need extra help or as a whole class activity to review the material covered.

MAGIC SQUARES

The magic squares not only reinforce the material covered but also work on reasoning and math skills. Many teachers have told us that their students really enjoy doing these!

WORD SEARCH PUZZLES

The word search words go in all directions, as indicated on your answer keys. Two of the word search puzzles have the clues listed rather than the words. This makes the puzzle a little more difficult, but it reinforces the material better. Two word search puzzles have words only for students who find the clue puzzles too difficult.

CROSSWORD PUZZLES

Both unit and vocabulary word sections have 4 crossword puzzles.

BINGO CARDS

There are 32 individual bingo cards for the unit words and 32 individual bingo cards for the vocabulary words. You can use your word list as a "call list," calling the words at random and marking them off of your list as you go, or you could use the flash cards by cutting them apart and drawing the words at random from a hat (or box or whatever). To make a better review, you might ask for the definition and spelling of each word as you call it out–or you could call out the definitions and have students tell you the words they need to look for on the puzzle.

JUGGLE LETTERS

The vocabulary juggle letter game is intended to help students learn the spellings of the words. One sheet has the definitions listed on it as an extra help for students who need it or to reinforce the definitions if you choose to do so.

FLASH CARDS

We've included a set of vocabulary flash cards you can duplicate, cut, and fold for your students. Some teachers make a few sets for general use by the class; others make a set for each student. Some teachers duplicate them for each student and have the students cut & fold their own. You can cut out just the words and put them in a hat, have each student pick out one word and write the definition and a sentence for that word. Students then swap words and papers, with the next student adding a sentence of his own under the last one. You can have students swap as many times as you like. Each time the student will read the sentences written prior to his own and then add a sentence. You can cut out the words and definitions separately and play "I Have; Who Has?" Each student in the room draws a word and definition. The first student says, "I have (the name of the word). Who has the definition?" The student with the definition reads it then says, "I have (the name of the vocabulary word she has). Who has the definition?" The round continues until all words and definitions have been given.

That Was Then, This Is Now Word List

No.	Word	Clue/Definition
1.	ANGELA	Mark cut her hair to get even for the fight
2.	AUTHORITY	Bryon had never been able to accept it
3.	BERNARD	Bryon thought he resembled one: St. ___
4.	BOTTLE	Weapon used on Mark's head
5.	BRYON	Looked like a Saint Bernard puppy
6.	CAR	Bryon was given Charlie's
7.	CARLSON	M&M and Cathy's last name
8.	CAT	Mark's hippie nickname
9.	CATHY	An innocent chick
10.	CHARLIE	Saved Mark's and Bryon's lives
11.	CONNIE	Told her friends to kill Mike
12.	CORVETTE	These riders made an obscene remark
13.	COWBOY	Mark's real father
14.	CURLY	Tried to jump M&M
15.	CURTIS	Unknowing object of Angela's affections
16.	DANCE	Bryon and Cathy's first date
17.	DAVE	Dirty ___ had brass knuckles
18.	DOUGLAS	Bryon's last name
19.	FATHER	M&M's criticized his hair and grades
20.	FREAK	M&M's hippie nickname: Baby ___
21.	GALAHAD	Mike described himself this way: Sir ___
22.	HAIR	Reason for Bryon's beating by the Shephards
23.	HOSPITAL	Bryon's mother was here for a while
24.	HUSTLER	Bryon's pool talent
25.	LIE	Bryon did this a lot, according to Charlie
26.	LION	Mark resembled one
27.	M&M	He ran away from home
28.	MARK	He looked like a friendly lion
29.	MIKE	He was beaten for defending a black girl
30.	MOTHER	Bryon's was in the hospital
31.	PEACE	M&M wore this medallion
32.	PILLS	Mark was selling them
33.	POOL	Bryon's game
34.	PRINCIPAL	Mark borrowed his car
35.	RANDY	Van-driving hippie college student
36.	RIBBON	The kids drove up and down here
37.	SHEPHARD	Angela and Curly's last name
38.	SHOTGUN	Charlie used one to protect the boys
39.	SOCS	Invited Bryon to their parties
40.	SPIDERS	M&M saw them on his bad trip
41.	STEALING	It was the same as buying, according to Mark
42.	STUPID	Mark thought Mike was ___
43.	TERRY	Short; round; a real nut: ___ Jones
44.	TEXANS	Wanted to get even with Bryon and Mark
45.	TIM	Leader of the Shephard gang
46.	WIRING	Mark's car talent: Hot-___

That Was Then, This Is Now Fill In The Blanks 1

_____ 1. Unknowing object of Angela's affections

_____ 2. Bryon thought he resembled one: St. ___

_____ 3. Tried to jump M&M

_____ 4. Told her friends to kill Mike

_____ 5. Mark resembled one

_____ 6. Bryon had never been able to accept it

_____ 7. Van-driving hippie college student

_____ 8. Short; round; a real nut: ___ Jones

_____ 9. Charlie used one to protect the boys

_____ 10. M&M and Cathy's last name

_____ 11. Bryon's pool talent

_____ 12. Bryon's last name

_____ 13. Weapon used on Mark's head

_____ 14. Angela and Curly's last name

_____ 15. It was the same as buying, according to Mark

_____ 16. Wanted to get even with Bryon and Mark

_____ 17. Reason for Bryon's beating by the Shephards

_____ 18. Saved Mark's and Bryon's lives

_____ 19. He looked like a friendly lion

_____ 20. Mark borrowed his car

That Was Then, This Is Now Fill In The Blanks 1 Answer Key

CURTIS	1. Unknowing object of Angela's affections
BERNARD	2. Bryon thought he resembled one: St. ___
CURLY	3. Tried to jump M&M
CONNIE	4. Told her friends to kill Mike
LION	5. Mark resembled one
AUTHORITY	6. Bryon had never been able to accept it
RANDY	7. Van-driving hippie college student
TERRY	8. Short; round; a real nut: ___ Jones
SHOTGUN	9. Charlie used one to protect the boys
CARLSON	10. M&M and Cathy's last name
HUSTLER	11. Bryon's pool talent
DOUGLAS	12. Bryon's last name
BOTTLE	13. Weapon used on Mark's head
SHEPHARD	14. Angela and Curly's last name
STEALING	15. It was the same as buying, according to Mark
TEXANS	16. Wanted to get even with Bryon and Mark
HAIR	17. Reason for Bryon's beating by the Shephards
CHARLIE	18. Saved Mark's and Bryon's lives
MARK	19. He looked like a friendly lion
PRINCIPAL	20. Mark borrowed his car

That Was Then, This Is Now Fill In The Blanks 2

_____ 1. Van-driving hippie college student

_____ 2. Mark's real father

_____ 3. Leader of the Shepherd gang

_____ 4. Wanted to get even with Bryon and Mark

_____ 5. Bryon and Cathy's first date

_____ 6. Mark borrowed his car

_____ 7. Mark resembled one

_____ 8. Bryon's was in the hospital

_____ 9. Dirty ___ had brass knuckles

_____ 10. Mark was selling them

_____ 11. M&M saw them on his bad trip

_____ 12. Bryon thought he resembled one: St. ___

_____ 13. Unknowing object of Angela's affections

_____ 14. Mike described himself this way: Sir ___

_____ 15. Bryon's game

_____ 16. He was beaten for defending a black girl

_____ 17. Short; round; a real nut: ___ Jones

_____ 18. M&M and Cathy's last name

_____ 19. He ran away from home

_____ 20. It was the same as buying, according to Mark

That Was Then, This Is Now Fill In The Blanks 2 Answer Key

RANDY	1. Van-driving hippie college student
COWBOY	2. Mark's real father
TIM	3. Leader of the Shepherd gang
TEXANS	4. Wanted to get even with Bryon and Mark
DANCE	5. Bryon and Cathy's first date
PRINCIPAL	6. Mark borrowed his car
LION	7. Mark resembled one
MOTHER	8. Bryon's was in the hospital
DAVE	9. Dirty ___ had brass knuckles
PILLS	10. Mark was selling them
SPIDERS	11. M&M saw them on his bad trip
BERNARD	12. Bryon thought he resembled one: St. ___
CURTIS	13. Unknowing object of Angela's affections
GALAHAD	14. Mike described himself this way: Sir ___
POOL	15. Bryon's game
MIKE	16. He was beaten for defending a black girl
TERRY	17. Short; round; a real nut: ___ Jones
CARLSON	18. M&M and Cathy's last name
M&M	19. He ran away from home
STEALING	20. It was the same as buying, according to Mark

That Was Then, This Is Now Fill In The Blanks 3

1. He ran away from home
2. Mark thought Mike was ___
3. Bryon's was in the hospital
4. Bryon had never been able to accept it
5. M&M and Cathy's last name
6. The kids drove up and down here
7. Mark's car talent: Hot-___
8. Bryon thought he resembled one: St. ___
9. Reason for Bryon's beating by the Shephards
10. Invited Bryon to their parties
11. It was the same as buying, according to Mark
12. Saved Mark's and Bryon's lives
13. Dirty ___ had brass knuckles
14. Bryon did this a lot, according to Charlie
15. He was beaten for defending a black girl
16. Short; round; a real nut: ___ Jones
17. An innocent chick
18. These riders made an obscene remark
19. Unknowing object of Angela's affections
20. M&M's hippie nickname: Baby ___

That Was Then, This Is Now Fill In The Blanks 3 Answer Key

M&M	1. He ran away from home
STUPID	2. Mark thought Mike was ___
MOTHER	3. Bryon's ___ was in the hospital
AUTHORITY	4. Bryon had never been able to accept it
CARLSON	5. M&M and Cathy's last name
RIBBON	6. The kids drove up and down here
WIRING	7. Mark's car talent: Hot-___
BERNARD	8. Bryon thought he resembled one: St. ___
HAIR	9. Reason for Bryon's beating by the Shephards
SOCS	10. Invited Bryon to their parties
STEALING	11. It was the same as buying, according to Mark
CHARLIE	12. Saved Mark's and Bryon's lives
DAVE	13. Dirty ___ had brass knuckles
LIE	14. Bryon did this a lot, according to Charlie
MIKE	15. He was beaten for defending a black girl
TERRY	16. Short; round; a real nut: ___ Jones
CATHY	17. An innocent chick
CORVETTE	18. These riders made an obscene remark
CURTIS	19. Unknowing object of Angela's affections
FREAK	20. M&M's hippie nickname: Baby ___

That Was Then, This Is Now Fill In The Blanks 4

_____ 1. He was beaten for defending a black girl

_____ 2. Told her friends to kill Mike

_____ 3. Bryon's last name

_____ 4. Weapon used on Mark's head

_____ 5. These riders made an obscene remark

_____ 6. M&M's criticized his hair and grades

_____ 7. Bryon did this a lot, according to Charlie

_____ 8. Invited Bryon to their parties

_____ 9. Angela and Curly's last name

_____ 10. Bryon thought he resembled one: St. ___

_____ 11. Wanted to get even with Bryon and Mark

_____ 12. An innocent chick

_____ 13. Bryon and Cathy's first date

_____ 14. Mark thought Mike was ___

_____ 15. Mark was selling them

_____ 16. It was the same as buying, according to Mark

_____ 17. M&M saw them on his bad trip

_____ 18. Leader of the Shepherd gang

_____ 19. He ran away from home

_____ 20. Mark borrowed his car

That Was Then, This Is Now Fill In The Blanks 4 Answer Key

MIKE	1. He was beaten for defending a black girl
CONNIE	2. Told her friends to kill Mike
DOUGLAS	3. Bryon's last name
BOTTLE	4. Weapon used on Mark's head
CORVETTE	5. These riders made an obscene remark
FATHER	6. M&M's criticized his hair and grades
LIE	7. Bryon did this a lot, according to Charlie
SOCS	8. Invited Bryon to their parties
SHEPHARD	9. Angela and Curly's last name
BERNARD	10. Bryon thought he resembled one: St. ___
TEXANS	11. Wanted to get even with Bryon and Mark
CATHY	12. An innocent chick
DANCE	13. Bryon and Cathy's first date
STUPID	14. Mark thought Mike was ___
PILLS	15. Mark was selling them
STEALING	16. It was the same as buying, according to Mark
SPIDERS	17. M&M saw them on his bad trip
TIM	18. Leader of the Shepherd gang
M&M	19. He ran away from home
PRINCIPAL	20. Mark borrowed his car

That Was Then, This Is Now Matching 1

___ 1. CAT   A. Bryon's last name
___ 2. WIRING   B. Angela and Curly's last name
___ 3. CATHY   C. Leader of the Shepherd gang
___ 4. SHEPHARD   D. Bryon's was in the hospital
___ 5. CONNIE   E. M&M saw them on his bad trip
___ 6. LIE   F. An innocent chick
___ 7. POOL   G. Bryon had never been able to accept it
___ 8. SPIDERS   H. He ran away from home
___ 9. STEALING   I. Mark was selling them
___10. LION   J. Mike described himself this way: Sir ___
___11. AUTHORITY   K. The kids drove up and down here
___12. COWBOY   L. Mark's car talent: Hot-___
___13. CHARLIE   M. Mark's real father
___14. GALAHAD   N. M&M and Cathy's last name
___15. TERRY   O. Bryon's game
___16. CARLSON   P. Reason for Bryon's beating by the Shephards
___17. CURLY   Q. Mark resembled one
___18. DOUGLAS   R. Saved Mark's and Bryon's lives
___19. M&M   S. Tried to jump M&M
___20. RIBBON   T. It was the same as buying, according to Mark
___21. PILLS   U. He was beaten for defending a black girl
___22. MOTHER   V. Short; round; a real nut: ___ Jones
___23. HAIR   W. Told her friends to kill Mike
___24. MIKE   X. Mark's hippie nickname
___25. TIM   Y. Bryon did this a lot, according to Charlie

That Was Then, This Is Now Matching 1 Answer Key

X - 1. CAT
L - 2. WIRING
F - 3. CATHY
B - 4. SHEPHARD
W - 5. CONNIE
Y - 6. LIE
O - 7. POOL
E - 8. SPIDERS
T - 9. STEALING
Q - 10. LION
G - 11. AUTHORITY
M - 12. COWBOY
R - 13. CHARLIE
J - 14. GALAHAD
V - 15. TERRY
N - 16. CARLSON
S - 17. CURLY
A - 18. DOUGLAS
H - 19. M&M
K - 20. RIBBON
I - 21. PILLS
D - 22. MOTHER
P - 23. HAIR
U - 24. MIKE
C - 25. TIM

A. Bryon's last name
B. Angela and Curly's last name
C. Leader of the Shepherd gang
D. Bryon's was in the hospital
E. M&M saw them on his bad trip
F. An innocent chick
G. Bryon had never been able to accept it
H. He ran away from home
I. Mark was selling them
J. Mike described himself this way: Sir ___
K. The kids drove up and down here
L. Mark's car talent: Hot-___
M. Mark's real father
N. M&M and Cathy's last name
O. Bryon's game
P. Reason for Bryon's beating by the Shephards
Q. Mark resembled one
R. Saved Mark's and Bryon's lives
S. Tried to jump M&M
T. It was the same as buying, according to Mark
U. He was beaten for defending a black girl
V. Short; round; a real nut: ___ Jones
W. Told her friends to kill Mike
X. Mark's hippie nickname
Y. Bryon did this a lot, according to Charlie

That Was Then, This Is Now Matching 2

___ 1. DOUGLAS   A. It was the same as buying, according to Mark
___ 2. TERRY   B. M&M's criticized his hair and grades
___ 3. HOSPITAL   C. Bryon had never been able to accept it
___ 4. MARK   D. Mark's hippie nickname
___ 5. CAT   E. Unknowing object of Angela's affections
___ 6. MIKE   F. Saved Mark's and Bryon's lives
___ 7. STEALING   G. Mark resembled one
___ 8. DANCE   H. He looked like a friendly lion
___ 9. HAIR   I. He was beaten for defending a black girl
___10. FATHER   J. Bryon's pool talent
___11. CHARLIE   K. Bryon did this a lot, according to Charlie
___12. SHEPHARD   L. Bryon's mother was here for a while
___13. LIE   M. Bryon's was in the hospital
___14. BOTTLE   N. Short; round; a real nut: ___ Jones
___15. RANDY   O. Weapon used on Mark's head
___16. MOTHER   P. Bryon and Cathy's first date
___17. AUTHORITY   Q. Bryon was given Charlie's
___18. LION   R. Van-driving hippie college student
___19. WIRING   S. Mark's car talent: Hot-___
___20. CONNIE   T. These riders made an obscene remark
___21. CORVETTE   U. Bryon's last name
___22. CURTIS   V. Charlie used one to protect the boys
___23. HUSTLER   W. Angela and Curly's last name
___24. CAR   X. Told her friends to kill Mike
___25. SHOTGUN   Y. Reason for Bryon's beating by the Shephards

That Was Then, This Is Now Matching 2 Answer Key

U - 1. DOUGLAS	A. It was the same as buying, according to Mark
N - 2. TERRY	B. M&M's criticized his hair and grades
L - 3. HOSPITAL	C. Bryon had never been able to accept it
H - 4. MARK	D. Mark's hippie nickname
D - 5. CAT	E. Unknowing object of Angela's affections
I - 6. MIKE	F. Saved Mark's and Bryon's lives
A - 7. STEALING	G. Mark resembled one
P - 8. DANCE	H. He looked like a friendly lion
Y - 9. HAIR	I. He was beaten for defending a black girl
B - 10. FATHER	J. Bryon's pool talent
F - 11. CHARLIE	K. Bryon did this a lot, according to Charlie
W - 12. SHEPHARD	L. Bryon's mother was here for a while
K - 13. LIE	M. Bryon's was in the hospital
O - 14. BOTTLE	N. Short; round; a real nut: ___ Jones
R - 15. RANDY	O. Weapon used on Mark's head
M - 16. MOTHER	P. Bryon and Cathy's first date
C - 17. AUTHORITY	Q. Bryon was given Charlie's
G - 18. LION	R. Van-driving hippie college student
S - 19. WIRING	S. Mark's car talent: Hot-___
X - 20. CONNIE	T. These riders made an obscene remark
T - 21. CORVETTE	U. Bryon's last name
E - 22. CURTIS	V. Charlie used one to protect the boys
J - 23. HUSTLER	W. Angela and Curly's last name
Q - 24. CAR	X. Told her friends to kill Mike
V - 25. SHOTGUN	Y. Reason for Bryon's beating by the Shephards

That Was Then, This Is Now Matching 3

___ 1. POOL A. Mark cut her hair to get even for the fight
___ 2. BOTTLE B. Bryon's game
___ 3. WIRING C. Tried to jump M&M
___ 4. PEACE D. Bryon had never been able to accept it
___ 5. COWBOY E. Invited Bryon to their parties
___ 6. PRINCIPAL F. He was beaten for defending a black girl
___ 7. TIM G. Angela and Curly's last name
___ 8. TEXANS H. Wanted to get even with Bryon and Mark
___ 9. MOTHER I. Looked like a Saint Bernard puppy
___10. STUPID J. Dirty ___ had brass knuckles
___11. GALAHAD K. It was the same as buying, according to Mark
___12. DANCE L. Weapon used on Mark's head
___13. STEALING M. Mark's car talent: Hot-___
___14. SPIDERS N. Bryon and Cathy's first date
___15. BERNARD O. Leader of the Shepherd gang
___16. MIKE P. Mark's real father
___17. HOSPITAL Q. M&M saw them on his bad trip
___18. BRYON R. Mark thought Mike was ___
___19. AUTHORITY S. Mark borrowed his car
___20. CURLY T. Mike described himself this way: Sir ___
___21. ANGELA U. Bryon's was in the hospital
___22. SHEPHARD V. Bryon's mother was here for a while
___23. TERRY W. Short; round; a real nut: ___ Jones
___24. DAVE X. M&M wore this medallion
___25. SOCS Y. Bryon thought he resembled one: St. ___

That Was Then, This Is Now Matching 3 Answer Key

B - 1. POOL	A.	Mark cut her hair to get even for the fight
L - 2. BOTTLE	B.	Bryon's game
M - 3. WIRING	C.	Tried to jump M&M
X - 4. PEACE	D.	Bryon had never been able to accept it
P - 5. COWBOY	E.	Invited Bryon to their parties
S - 6. PRINCIPAL	F.	He was beaten for defending a black girl
O - 7. TIM	G.	Angela and Curly's last name
H - 8. TEXANS	H.	Wanted to get even with Bryon and Mark
U - 9. MOTHER	I.	Looked like a Saint Bernard puppy
R -10. STUPID	J.	Dirty ___ had brass knuckles
T -11. GALAHAD	K.	It was the same as buying, according to Mark
N -12. DANCE	L.	Weapon used on Mark's head
K -13. STEALING	M.	Mark's car talent: Hot-___
Q -14. SPIDERS	N.	Bryon and Cathy's first date
Y -15. BERNARD	O.	Leader of the Shepherd gang
F -16. MIKE	P.	Mark's real father
V -17. HOSPITAL	Q.	M&M saw them on his bad trip
I - 18. BRYON	R.	Mark thought Mike was ___
D -19. AUTHORITY	S.	Mark borrowed his car
C -20. CURLY	T.	Mike described himself this way: Sir ___
A -21. ANGELA	U.	Bryon's was in the hospital
G -22. SHEPHARD	V.	Bryon's mother was here for a while
W -23. TERRY	W.	Short; round; a real nut: ___ Jones
J - 24. DAVE	X.	M&M wore this medallion
E -25. SOCS	Y.	Bryon thought he resembled one: St. ___

That Was Then, This Is Now Matching 4

___ 1. GALAHAD
___ 2. HUSTLER
___ 3. RANDY
___ 4. COWBOY
___ 5. CHARLIE
___ 6. TIM
___ 7. WIRING
___ 8. CAT
___ 9. SOCS
___ 10. CONNIE
___ 11. CURLY
___ 12. SHEPHARD
___ 13. DAVE
___ 14. LIE
___ 15. DANCE
___ 16. CATHY
___ 17. STUPID
___ 18. LION
___ 19. POOL
___ 20. FATHER
___ 21. MOTHER
___ 22. M&M
___ 23. ANGELA
___ 24. TERRY
___ 25. STEALING

A. Short; round; a real nut: ___ Jones
B. Van-driving hippie college student
C. Tried to jump M&M
D. Bryon and Cathy's first date
E. Saved Mark's and Bryon's lives
F. Bryon's game
G. Mark thought Mike was ___
H. It was the same as buying, according to Mark
I. Mark resembled one
J. Leader of the Shepherd gang
K. Bryon's pool talent
L. Invited Bryon to their parties
M. He ran away from home
N. M&M's criticized his hair and grades
O. Mark's hippie nickname
P. Dirty ___ had brass knuckles
Q. Mark's car talent: Hot-___
R. An innocent chick
S. Mark's real father
T. Mike described himself this way: Sir ___
U. Bryon did this a lot, according to Charlie
V. Bryon's was in the hospital
W. Mark cut her hair to get even for the fight
X. Angela and Curly's last name
Y. Told her friends to kill Mike

That Was Then, This Is Now Matching 4 Answer Key

T - 1. GALAHAD	A.	Short; round; a real nut: ___ Jones
K - 2. HUSTLER	B.	Van-driving hippie college student
B - 3. RANDY	C.	Tried to jump M&M
S - 4. COWBOY	D.	Bryon and Cathy's first date
E - 5. CHARLIE	E.	Saved Mark's and Bryon's lives
J - 6. TIM	F.	Bryon's game
Q - 7. WIRING	G.	Mark thought Mike was ___
O - 8. CAT	H.	It was the same as buying, according to Mark
L - 9. SOCS	I.	Mark resembled one
Y -10. CONNIE	J.	Leader of the Shepherd gang
C -11. CURLY	K.	Bryon's pool talent
X -12. SHEPHARD	L.	Invited Bryon to their parties
P -13. DAVE	M.	He ran away from home
U -14. LIE	N.	M&M's criticized his hair and grades
D -15. DANCE	O.	Mark's hippie nickname
R -16. CATHY	P.	Dirty ___ had brass knuckles
G -17. STUPID	Q.	Mark's car talent: Hot-___
I - 18. LION	R.	An innocent chick
F -19. POOL	S.	Mark's real father
N -20. FATHER	T.	Mike described himself this way: Sir ___
V -21. MOTHER	U.	Bryon did this a lot, according to Charlie
M -22. M&M	V.	Bryon's was in the hospital
W -23. ANGELA	W.	Mark cut her hair to get even for the fight
A -24. TERRY	X.	Angela and Curly's last name
H -25. STEALING	Y.	Told her friends to kill Mike

That Was Then, This Is Now Magic Squares 1

Match the definition with the vocabulary word. Put your answers in the magic squares below. When your answers are correct, all columns and rows will add to the same number.

A. MARK   E. FREAK   I. DOUGLAS   M. SHOTGUN
B. CAR   F. CATHY   J. AUTHORITY N. STUPID
C. MIKE   G. CURLY   K. CHARLIE   O. LION
D. WIRING H. CAT   L. BERNARD   P. PRINCIPAL

1. Charlie used one to protect the boys
2. An innocent chick
3. Mark's hippie nickname
4. Mark resembled one
5. Bryon thought he resembled one: St. ___
6. He was beaten for defending a black girl
7. He looked like a friendly lion
8. Bryon had never been able to accept it
9. Saved Mark's and Bryon's lives
10. Mark's car talent: Hot-___
11. Bryon was given Charlie's
12. Bryon's last name
13. Mark thought Mike was ___
14. M&M's hippie nickname: Baby ___
15. Tried to jump M&M
16. Mark borrowed his car

A=	B=	C=	D=
E=	F=	G=	H=
I=	J=	K=	L=
M=	N=	O=	P=

That Was Then, This Is Now Magic Squares 1 Answer Key

Match the definition with the vocabulary word. Put your answers in the magic squares below. When your answers are correct, all columns and rows will add to the same number.

A. MARK
B. CAR
C. MIKE
D. WIRING
E. FREAK
F. CATHY
G. CURLY
H. CAT
I. DOUGLAS
J. AUTHORITY
K. CHARLIE
L. BERNARD
M. SHOTGUN
N. STUPID
O. LION
P. PRINCIPAL

1. Charlie used one to protect the boys
2. An innocent chick
3. Mark's hippie nickname
4. Mark resembled one
5. Bryon thought he resembled one: St. ___
6. He was beaten for defending a black girl
7. He looked like a friendly lion
8. Bryon had never been able to accept it
9. Saved Mark's and Bryon's lives
10. Mark's car talent: Hot-___
11. Bryon was given Charlie's
12. Bryon's last name
13. Mark thought Mike was ___
14. M&M's hippie nickname: Baby ___
15. Tried to jump M&M
16. Mark borrowed his car

A=7	B=11	C=6	D=10
E=14	F=2	G=15	H=3
I=12	J=8	K=9	L=5
M=1	N=13	O=4	P=16

That Was Then, This Is Now Magic Squares 2

Match the definition with the vocabulary word. Put your answers in the magic squares below. When your answers are correct, all columns and rows will add to the same number.

A. AUTHORITY   E. SOCS   I. CURLY   M. PRINCIPAL
B. COWBOY   F. MIKE   J. HOSPITAL   N. WIRING
C. POOL   G. PILLS   K. TERRY   O. LIE
D. CURTIS   H. CORVETTE L. PEACE   P. RANDY

1. Bryon had never been able to accept it
2. Mark's car talent: Hot-___
3. Bryon's mother was here for a while
4. Invited Bryon to their parties
5. Mark was selling them
6. M&M wore this medallion
7. Van-driving hippie college student
8. Bryon's game
9. Bryon did this a lot, according to Charlie
10. Unknowing object of Angela's affections
11. These riders made an obscene remark
12. Short; round; a real nut: ___ Jones
13. Tried to jump M&M
14. He was beaten for defending a black girl
15. Mark's real father
16. Mark borrowed his car

A=	B=	C=	D=
E=	F=	G=	H=
I=	J=	K=	L=
M=	N=	O=	P=

23
Copyrighted

That Was Then, This Is Now Magic Squares 2 Answer Key

Match the definition with the vocabulary word. Put your answers in the magic squares below. When your answers are correct, all columns and rows will add to the same number.

A. AUTHORITY   E. SOCS   I. CURLY   M. PRINCIPAL
B. COWBOY   F. MIKE   J. HOSPITAL   N. WIRING
C. POOL   G. PILLS   K. TERRY   O. LIE
D. CURTIS   H. CORVETTE   L. PEACE   P. RANDY

1. Bryon had never been able to accept it
2. Mark's car talent: Hot-___
3. Bryon's mother was here for a while
4. Invited Bryon to their parties
5. Mark was selling them
6. M&M wore this medallion
7. Van-driving hippie college student
8. Bryon's game
9. Bryon did this a lot, according to Charlie
10. Unknowing object of Angela's affections
11. These riders made an obscene remark
12. Short; round; a real nut: ___ Jones
13. Tried to jump M&M
14. He was beaten for defending a black girl
15. Mark's real father
16. Mark borrowed his car

A=1	B=15	C=8	D=10
E=4	F=14	G=5	H=11
I=13	J=3	K=12	L=6
M=16	N=2	O=9	P=7

24
Copyrighted

That Was Then, This Is Now Magic Squares 3

Match the definition with the vocabulary word. Put your answers in the magic squares below. When your answers are correct, all columns and rows will add to the same number.

A. RIBBON
B. FATHER
C. BRYON
D. DOUGLAS
E. HAIR
F. CHARLIE
G. CONNIE
H. RANDY
I. ANGELA
J. MOTHER
K. SPIDERS
L. MARK
M. CATHY
N. PRINCIPAL
O. POOL
P. AUTHORITY

1. Bryon's game
2. Bryon's last name
3. Bryon's was in the hospital
4. Reason for Bryon's beating by the Shephards
5. Mark cut her hair to get even for the fight
6. Saved Mark's and Bryon's lives
7. Bryon had never been able to accept it
8. Looked like a Saint Bernard puppy
9. Van-driving hippie college student
10. M&M saw them on his bad trip
11. The kids drove up and down here
12. Mark borrowed his car
13. M&M's criticized his hair and grades
14. An innocent chick
15. Told her friends to kill Mike
16. He looked like a friendly lion

A=	B=	C=	D=
E=	F=	G=	H=
I=	J=	K=	L=
M=	N=	O=	P=

25
Copyrighted

That Was Then, This Is Now Magic Squares 3 Answer Key

Match the definition with the vocabulary word. Put your answers in the magic squares below. When your answers are correct, all columns and rows will add to the same number.

A. RIBBON
B. FATHER
C. BRYON
D. DOUGLAS
E. HAIR
F. CHARLIE
G. CONNIE
H. RANDY
I. ANGELA
J. MOTHER
K. SPIDERS
L. MARK
M. CATHY
N. PRINCIPAL
O. POOL
P. AUTHORITY

1. Bryon's game
2. Bryon's last name
3. Bryon's was in the hospital
4. Reason for Bryon's beating by the Shephards
5. Mark cut her hair to get even for the fight
6. Saved Mark's and Bryon's lives
7. Bryon had never been able to accept it
8. Looked like a Saint Bernard puppy
9. Van-driving hippie college student
10. M&M saw them on his bad trip
11. The kids drove up and down here
12. Mark borrowed his car
13. M&M's criticized his hair and grades
14. An innocent chick
15. Told her friends to kill Mike
16. He looked like a friendly lion

A=11	B=13	C=8	D=2
E=4	F=6	G=15	H=9
I=5	J=3	K=10	L=16
M=14	N=12	O=1	P=7

That Was Then, This Is Now Magic Squares 4

Match the definition with the vocabulary word. Put your answers in the magic squares below. When your answers are correct, all columns and rows will add to the same number.

A. STEALING   E. CURTIS   I. DANCE   M. CAT
B. RANDY   F. STUPID   J. SHOTGUN   N. CAR
C. LION   G. TIM   K. HUSTLER   O. M&M
D. DOUGLAS   H. PILLS   L. WIRING   P. DAVE

1. Mark was selling them
2. It was the same as buying, according to Mark
3. Van-driving hippie college student
4. Leader of the Shepherd gang
5. Charlie used one to protect the boys
6. He ran away from home
7. Dirty ___ had brass knuckles
8. Bryon and Cathy's first date
9. Bryon's pool talent
10. Bryon was given Charlie's
11. Mark's hippie nickname
12. Mark's car talent: Hot-___
13. Unknowing object of Angela's affections
14. Bryon's last name
15. Mark resembled one
16. Mark thought Mike was ___

A=	B=	C=	D=
E=	F=	G=	H=
I=	J=	K=	L=
M=	N=	O=	P=

That Was Then, This Is Now Magic Squares 4 Answer Key

Match the definition with the vocabulary word. Put your answers in the magic squares below. When your answers are correct, all columns and rows will add to the same number.

A. STEALING   E. CURTIS   I. DANCE   M. CAT
B. RANDY   F. STUPID   J. SHOTGUN   N. CAR
C. LION   G. TIM   K. HUSTLER   O. M&M
D. DOUGLAS   H. PILLS   L. WIRING   P. DAVE

1. Mark was selling them
2. It was the same as buying, according to Mark
3. Van-driving hippie college student
4. Leader of the Shepherd gang
5. Charlie used one to protect the boys
6. He ran away from home
7. Dirty ___ had brass knuckles
8. Bryon and Cathy's first date
9. Bryon's pool talent
10. Bryon was given Charlie's
11. Mark's hippie nickname
12. Mark's car talent: Hot-___
13. Unknowing object of Angela's affections
14. Bryon's last name
15. Mark resembled one
16. Mark thought Mike was ___

A=2	B=3	C=15	D=14
E=13	F=16	G=4	H=1
I=8	J=5	K=9	L=12
M=11	N=10	O=6	P=7

That Was Then, This Is Now Word Search 1

Words are placed backwards, forward, diagonally, up and down. Clues listed below can help you find the words. Circle the hidden vocabulary words in the maze.

W	R	A	N	D	Y	Y	S	T	E	A	L	I	N	G	L	I	O	N	Y
S	I	F	C	T	A	K	D	P	P	D	H	F	F	A	Y	C	W	E	E
B	W	R	A	H	T	V	L	G	I	O	P	T	X	L	M	G	K	C	T
D	E	C	I	T	X	J	E	Y	C	D	O	N	C	A	R	I	A	F	R
S	A	R	L	N	H	B	R	Y	O	N	E	L	H	H	M	E	B	R	R
V	S	N	N	C	G	E	D	H	W	G	I	R	P	A	P	A	P	E	Q
F	T	L	C	A	C	V	R	T	B	N	N	H	S	D	S	N	R	A	C
J	U	Y	V	E	R	Y	A	G	O	C	N	P	N	G	A	W	B	K	D
W	P	B	M	A	K	D	H	J	Y	X	O	P	I	L	L	S	W	R	M
G	I	Z	Y	N	V	G	P	T	Z	J	C	C	N	B	G	N	B	J	J
H	D	X	W	G	S	H	E	G	N	Y	M	H	H	J	U	F	G	B	V
L	V	G	Q	E	C	S	H	P	Y	N	N	X	R	G	O	X	N	K	P
C	K	G	Y	L	F	W	S	N	X	X	Y	X	S	L	D	R	D	P	P
Y	N	Y	A	L	V	C	D	L	J	W	D	P	N	K	K	M	M	G	C
C	D	J	G	V	F	V	W	A	N	H	O	H	Q	J	F	X	L	J	W
O	K	B	M	W	M	M	D	P	N	O	O	G	Q	Q	R	T	Z	L	F
R	G	N	O	R	C	M	J	I	Y	S	S	P	C	F	R	V	P	V	N
V	X	S	T	C	T	E	V	C	G	L	P	T	V	Y	I	R	K	U	W
E	C	L	H	V	I	C	C	N	B	R	I	B	S	T	B	V	G	M	M
T	Y	U	E	L	H	G	A	I	V	A	T	N	S	S	B	T	H	T	F
T	E	R	R	Y	S	I	T	R	U	C	A	U	T	H	O	R	I	T	Y
E	T	A	Q	L	P	T	H	P	Y	X	L	C	L	H	N	C	I	K	N
H	H	G	L	J	Y	L	Y	H	E	P	S	A	S	I	M	M	S	Y	K
C	H	U	S	T	L	E	R	T	Y	B	O	T	T	L	E	H	A	I	R

An innocent chick (5)
Angela and Curly's last name (8)
Bryon and Cathy's first date (5)
Bryon did this a lot, according to Charlie (3)
Bryon had never been able to accept it (9)
Bryon thought he resembled one: St. ___ (7)
Bryon was given Charlie's (3)
Bryon's game (4)
Bryon's last name (7)
Bryon's mother was here for a while (8)
Bryon's pool talent (7)
Bryon's was in the hospital (6)
Charlie used one to protect the boys (7)
Dirty ___ had brass knuckles (4)
He looked like a friendly lion (4)
He was beaten for defending a black girl (4)
Invited Bryon to their parties (4)
It was the same as buying, according to Mark (8)
Leader of the Shepherd gang (3)
Looked like a Saint Bernard puppy (5)
M&M and Cathy's last name (7)
M&M saw them on his bad trip (7)
M&M wore this medallion (5)

M&M's criticized his hair and grades (6)
M&M's hippie nickname: Baby ___ (5)
Mark borrowed his car (9)
Mark cut her hair to get even for the fight (6)
Mark resembled one (4)
Mark thought Mike was ___ (6)
Mark was selling them (5)
Mark's car talent: Hot-___ (6)
Mark's hippie nickname (3)
Mark's real father (6)
Mike described himself this way: Sir ___ (7)
Reason for Bryon's beating by the Shephards (4)
Saved Mark's and Bryon's lives (7)
Short; round; a real nut: ___ Jones (5)
The kids drove up and down here (6)
These riders made an obscene remark (8)
Told her friends to kill Mike (6)
Tried to jump M&M (5)
Unknowing object of Angela's affections (6)
Van-driving hippie college student (5)
Wanted to get even with Bryon and Mark (6)
Weapon used on Mark's head (6)

That Was Then, This Is Now Word Search 1 Answer Key

Words are placed backwards, forward, diagonally, up and down. Clues listed below can help you find the words. Circle the hidden vocabulary words in the maze.

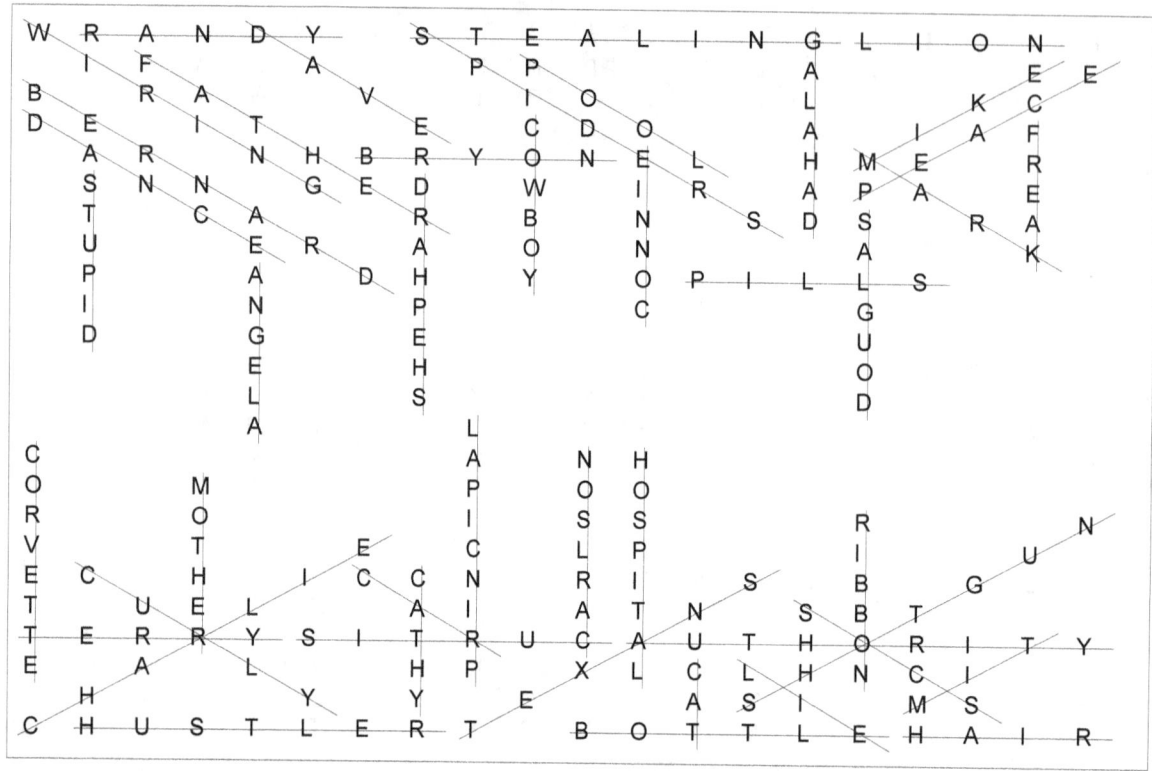

An innocent chick (5)
Angela and Curly's last name (8)
Bryon and Cathy's first date (5)
Bryon did this a lot, according to Charlie (3)
Bryon had never been able to accept it (9)
Bryon thought he resembled one: St. ___ (7)
Bryon was given Charlie's (3)
Bryon's game (4)
Bryon's last name (7)
Bryon's mother was here for a while (8)
Bryon's pool talent (7)
Bryon's was in the hospital (6)
Charlie used one to protect the boys (7)
Dirty ___ had brass knuckles (4)
He looked like a friendly lion (4)
He was beaten for defending a black girl (4)
Invited Bryon to their parties (4)
It was the same as buying, according to Mark (8)
Leader of the Shepherd gang (3)
Looked like a Saint Bernard puppy (5)
M&M and Cathy's last name (7)
M&M saw them on his bad trip (7)
M&M wore this medallion (5)

M&M's criticized his hair and grades (6)
M&M's hippie nickname: Baby ___ (5)
Mark borrowed his car (9)
Mark cut her hair to get even for the fight (6)
Mark resembled one (4)
Mark thought Mike was ___ (6)
Mark was selling them (5)
Mark's car talent: Hot-___ (6)
Mark's hippie nickname (3)
Mark's real father (6)
Mike described himself this way: Sir ___ (7)
Reason for Bryon's beating by the Shephards (4)
Saved Mark's and Bryon's lives (7)
Short; round; a real nut: ___ Jones (5)
The kids drove up and down here (6)
These riders made an obscene remark (8)
Told her friends to kill Mike (6)
Tried to jump M&M (5)
Unknowing object of Angela's affections (6)
Van-driving hippie college student (5)
Wanted to get even with Bryon and Mark (6)
Weapon used on Mark's head (6)

That Was Then, This Is Now Word Search 2

Words are placed backwards, forward, diagonally, up and down. Clues listed below can help you find the words. Circle the hidden vocabulary words in the maze.

```
C A T H A I R R C W B H D S T U P I D B
U A R O M K Z I A I R S O H P T B A E H
R S R S A P J B T R Y T U O V I N G V R
T O E P R S O B H I O T G T C C D B A F
I C H I K H F O Y N N R L G E U Z E D H
S S T T P E R N L G O E A U A X R R R J
Q C A A G P E H H K S L S N Z L A L H S
F H F L V H A W H J L T S P D N A N Y W
H A D V P A K J Y Y R S C Y R Y L H S Q
C R K T B R F Z O Q A U P E Q F I T A Q
V L B W N D K B V C C H B R Q Q O S Z D
G I K T M E W J R P M L A P I C N I R P
J E C X I O C E T Y F C H N M Q M H R V
H K G N C Y H H L F F R V A H Z T X K F
N W N B B T T S N F J R S U Z V B T Q Q
F O N T O O C K J P Q C S T K B N Y S N
C Y T M T T T D N E F M Y H X J P Q C E
V L S G M F M T M A H A Z O L M N J T F
Y L H K J F P L L C L F P R M I Z T K Q
Z B K S G N I L A E T S H I F T E R R Y
L Z M B J X Q F G V K W K T L V I L S W
W J Q Z V H F N R N B E K Y R L D M Y F
P X K P F X A D N N J T K O K R S C S J
G B P H Y X Y V M M Y N C V P J J J M D
```

An innocent chick (5)
Angela and Curly's last name (8)
Bryon and Cathy's first date (5)
Bryon did this a lot, according to Charlie (3)
Bryon had never been able to accept it (9)
Bryon thought he resembled one: St. ___ (7)
Bryon was given Charlie's (3)
Bryon's game (4)
Bryon's last name (7)
Bryon's mother was here for a while (8)
Bryon's pool talent (7)
Bryon's was in the hospital (6)
Charlie used one to protect the boys (7)
Dirty ___ had brass knuckles (4)
He looked like a friendly lion (4)
He was beaten for defending a black girl (4)
Invited Bryon to their parties (4)
It was the same as buying, according to Mark (8)
Leader of the Shepherd gang (3)
Looked like a Saint Bernard puppy (5)
M&M and Cathy's last name (7)
M&M saw them on his bad trip (7)
M&M wore this medallion (5)

M&M's criticized his hair and grades (6)
M&M's hippie nickname: Baby ___ (5)
Mark borrowed his car (9)
Mark cut her hair to get even for the fight (6)
Mark resembled one (4)
Mark thought Mike was ___ (6)
Mark was selling them (5)
Mark's car talent: Hot-___ (6)
Mark's hippie nickname (3)
Mark's real father (6)
Mike described himself this way: Sir ___ (7)
Reason for Bryon's beating by the Shephards (4)
Saved Mark's and Bryon's lives (7)
Short; round; a real nut: ___ Jones (5)
The kids drove up and down here (6)
These riders made an obscene remark (8)
Told her friends to kill Mike (6)
Tried to jump M&M (5)
Unknowing object of Angela's affections (6)
Van-driving hippie college student (5)
Wanted to get even with Bryon and Mark (6)
Weapon used on Mark's head (6)

That Was Then, This Is Now Word Search 2 Answer Key

Words are placed backwards, forward, diagonally, up and down. Clues listed below can help you find the words. Circle the hidden vocabulary words in the maze.

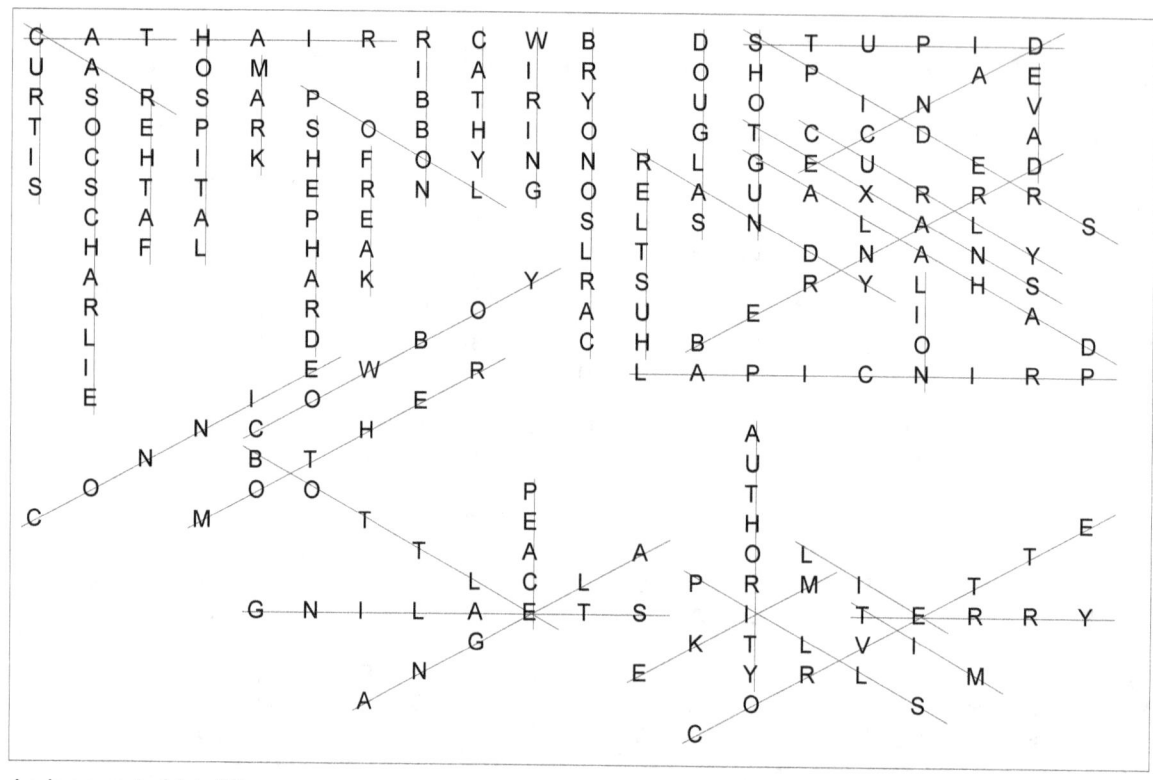

An innocent chick (5)
Angela and Curly's last name (8)
Bryon and Cathy's first date (5)
Bryon did this a lot, according to Charlie (3)
Bryon had never been able to accept it (9)
Bryon thought he resembled one: St. ___ (7)
Bryon was given Charlie's (3)
Bryon's game (4)
Bryon's last name (7)
Bryon's mother was here for a while (8)
Bryon's pool talent (7)
Bryon's was in the hospital (6)
Charlie used one to protect the boys (7)
Dirty ___ had brass knuckles (4)
He looked like a friendly lion (4)
He was beaten for defending a black girl (4)
Invited Bryon to their parties (4)
It was the same as buying, according to Mark (8)
Leader of the Shepherd gang (3)
Looked like a Saint Bernard puppy (5)
M&M and Cathy's last name (7)
M&M saw them on his bad trip (7)
M&M wore this medallion (5)

M&M's criticized his hair and grades (6)
M&M's hippie nickname: Baby ___ (5)
Mark borrowed his car (9)
Mark cut her hair to get even for the fight (6)
Mark resembled one (4)
Mark thought Mike was ___ (6)
Mark was selling them (5)
Mark's car talent: Hot-___ (6)
Mark's hippie nickname (3)
Mark's real father (6)
Mike described himself this way: Sir ___ (7)
Reason for Bryon's beating by the Shephards (4)
Saved Mark's and Bryon's lives (7)
Short; round; a real nut: ___ Jones (5)
The kids drove up and down here (6)
These riders made an obscene remark (8)
Told her friends to kill Mike (6)
Tried to jump M&M (5)
Unknowing object of Angela's affections (6)
Van-driving hippie college student (5)
Wanted to get even with Bryon and Mark (6)
Weapon used on Mark's head (6)

That Was Then, This Is Now Word Search 3

Words are placed backwards, forward, diagonally, up and down. Words listed below are included in the maze. Circle the hidden vocabulary words in the maze.

```
C J N H C W D A M A R K A E R F N H Y K
H N X X P N Y N M J L G D R G U D T J J
A F P V W N B G D D N R Y J G G I Q M Z
R Q R Y Z Y R E P Q B C W T H R P M G X
L Z X S X S Q L Y Q B C O D O Y T D G H
I W S R P E Y A C V X H T H S T K Q V N
E C K R I S N F S H S F T L T E P W N D
P Z J N M L N A K Z P U Z L H X R Q H Q
E Z N Y I S C T D H A S P B X A I F M X
A O V Z K L T H L V H C K X C N N L D X
C O R V E T T E L T T O B Z W S C Q I C
E O Y W W G T R A C D S G N M R I A C E
K L W R I Q C J B L V A Z G H I P T R W
B Z F B D R S X J S I S V Z H B A I D V
P O O L O L I O N D A N C E Y B L M R S
W R H L L Y T N J R N A G B H O N W A P
W A G W A X R P G A T K C W S N Q T H D
G N J L T V U L S N F P D P P J L Q P X
A D H A I R C C U R L Y I H U S T L E R
L Y Q D P J M M H E G D P L R G S T H K
A G H W S S L F M B E P U M L F G E S Y
H B W M O P Y B J R X X T X N S C R L K
A C A T H Y V K S R N O S L R A C R M H
D M O T H E R D O U G L A S J B R Y O N
```

ANGELA	CHARLIE	FATHER	MIKE	SHOTGUN
AUTHORITY	CONNIE	FREAK	MOTHER	SOCS
BERNARD	CORVETTE	GALAHAD	PEACE	SPIDERS
BOTTLE	COWBOY	HAIR	PILLS	STEALING
BRYON	CURLY	HOSPITAL	POOL	STUPID
CAR	CURTIS	HUSTLER	PRINCIPAL	TERRY
CARLSON	DANCE	LIE	RANDY	TEXANS
CAT	DAVE	LION	RIBBON	TIM
CATHY	DOUGLAS	MARK	SHEPHARD	WIRING

That Was Then, This Is Now Word Search 3 Answer Key

Words are placed backwards, forward, diagonally, up and down. Words listed below are included in the maze. Circle the hidden vocabulary words in the maze.

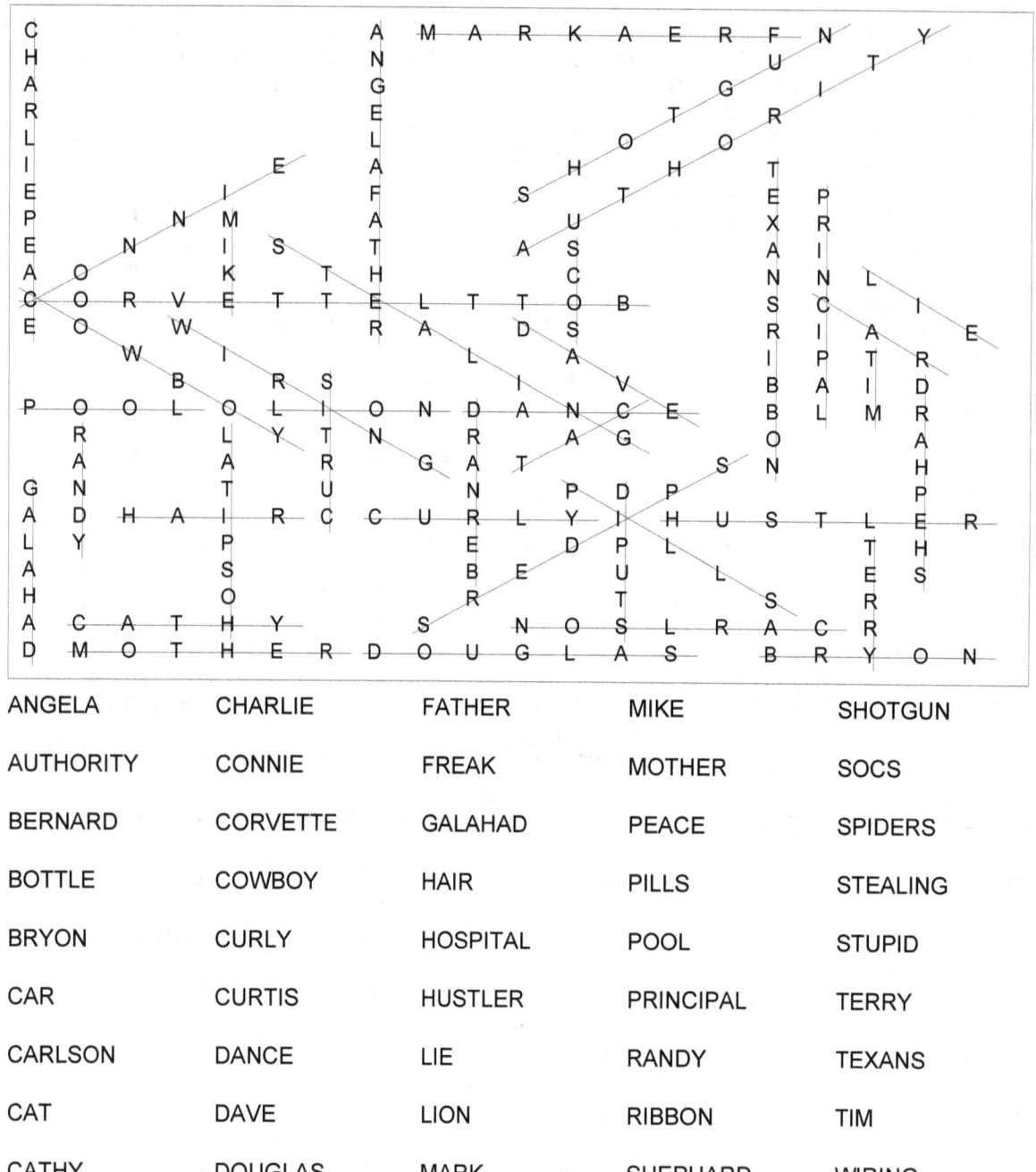

ANGELA	CHARLIE	FATHER	MIKE	SHOTGUN
AUTHORITY	CONNIE	FREAK	MOTHER	SOCS
BERNARD	CORVETTE	GALAHAD	PEACE	SPIDERS
BOTTLE	COWBOY	HAIR	PILLS	STEALING
BRYON	CURLY	HOSPITAL	POOL	STUPID
CAR	CURTIS	HUSTLER	PRINCIPAL	TERRY
CARLSON	DANCE	LIE	RANDY	TEXANS
CAT	DAVE	LION	RIBBON	TIM
CATHY	DOUGLAS	MARK	SHEPHARD	WIRING

That Was Then, This Is Now Word Search 4

Words are placed backwards, forward, diagonally, up and down. Words listed below are included in the maze. Circle the hidden vocabulary words in the maze.

```
P  I  L  L  S  V  S  W  S  J  C  C  A  T  T  V  T  C  Y  W
C  D  N  N  Y  I  B  H  C  W  D  A  Y  L  I  E  F  A  Z  S
H  R  R  B  T  R  K  B  O  J  N  N  T  R  L  M  R  R  B  Y
A  Q  T  R  B  A  L  O  H  T  T  W  E  H  Z  Q  G  R  D  G
R  C  U  P  E  Y  R  T  A  Q  G  H  P  W  Y  R  T  Q  Y  P
L  C  P  R  R  P  T  T  I  M  T  U  N  H  R  W  L  M  L  G
I  D  F  I  N  N  N  L  R  A  Q  S  N  R  P  B  R  G  K  P
E  O  T  N  A  V  W  E  F  K  N  T  V  G  K  G  B  K  C  L
B  U  G  C  R  S  T  U  P  I  D  L  S  T  E  A  L  I  N  G
R  G  W  I  D  S  P  Q  Y  W  L  E  N  V  C  Q  R  Q  D  J
Y  L  M  P  B  B  F  O  M  N  I  R  S  R  H  Y  K  A  S  S
O  A  R  A  S  J  B  Q  A  Y  A  R  X  B  J  N  H  B  P  G
N  S  D  L  C  W  G  B  R  D  U  S  I  M  D  A  N  C  I  Z
S  B  X  K  O  N  Y  B  K  D  T  L  P  N  L  W  T  O  D  G
R  H  H  C  W  D  N  F  C  N  H  G  C  A  G  J  R  R  E  P
T  T  E  T  H  X  O  J  V  Z  O  N  G  O  K  M  T  V  R  D
M  M  S  P  M  L  B  Q  K  Z  R  M  Q  H  N  Z  T  E  S  X
P  X  L  S  H  Q  B  M  C  L  I  N  O  G  N  Z  T  Z  A
X  O  I  S  D  A  I  A  J  K  T  K  V  S  L  J  I  T  L  F
P  M  O  T  H  E  R  A  N  D  Y  E  Y  P  E  A  C  E  D  S
Y  C  N  L  B  L  Q  D  G  P  A  L  G  I  V  C  G  X  A  G
S  W  K  W  S  F  G  K  P  S  R  V  L  T  G  N  Z  A  N  S
H  Z  B  O  M  M  P  K  X  U  G  Q  E  A  A  S  F  N  C  J
B  Q  N  Q  X  W  Y  L  C  C  P  N  J  L  K  Y  L  S  E  X
```

ANGELA	CHARLIE	FATHER	MIKE	SHOTGUN
AUTHORITY	CONNIE	FREAK	MOTHER	SOCS
BERNARD	CORVETTE	GALAHAD	PEACE	SPIDERS
BOTTLE	COWBOY	HAIR	PILLS	STEALING
BRYON	CURLY	HOSPITAL	POOL	STUPID
CAR	CURTIS	HUSTLER	PRINCIPAL	TERRY
CARLSON	DANCE	LIE	RANDY	TEXANS
CAT	DAVE	LION	RIBBON	TIM
CATHY	DOUGLAS	MARK	SHEPHARD	WIRING

That Was Then, This Is Now Word Search 4 Answer Key

Words are placed backwards, forward, diagonally, up and down. Words listed below are included in the maze. Circle the hidden vocabulary words in the maze.

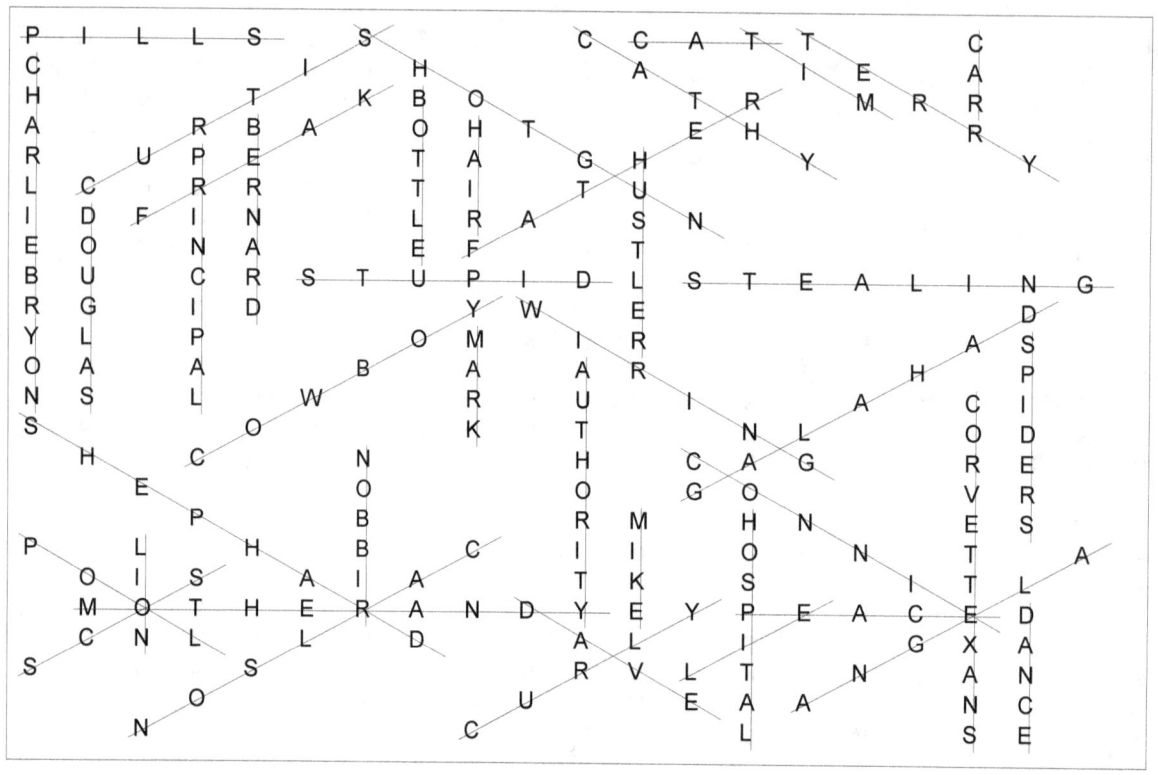

ANGELA	CHARLIE	FATHER	MIKE	SHOTGUN
AUTHORITY	CONNIE	FREAK	MOTHER	SOCS
BERNARD	CORVETTE	GALAHAD	PEACE	SPIDERS
BOTTLE	COWBOY	HAIR	PILLS	STEALING
BRYON	CURLY	HOSPITAL	POOL	STUPID
CAR	CURTIS	HUSTLER	PRINCIPAL	TERRY
CARLSON	DANCE	LIE	RANDY	TEXANS
CAT	DAVE	LION	RIBBON	TIM
CATHY	DOUGLAS	MARK	SHEPHARD	WIRING

That Was Then, This Is Now Crossword 1

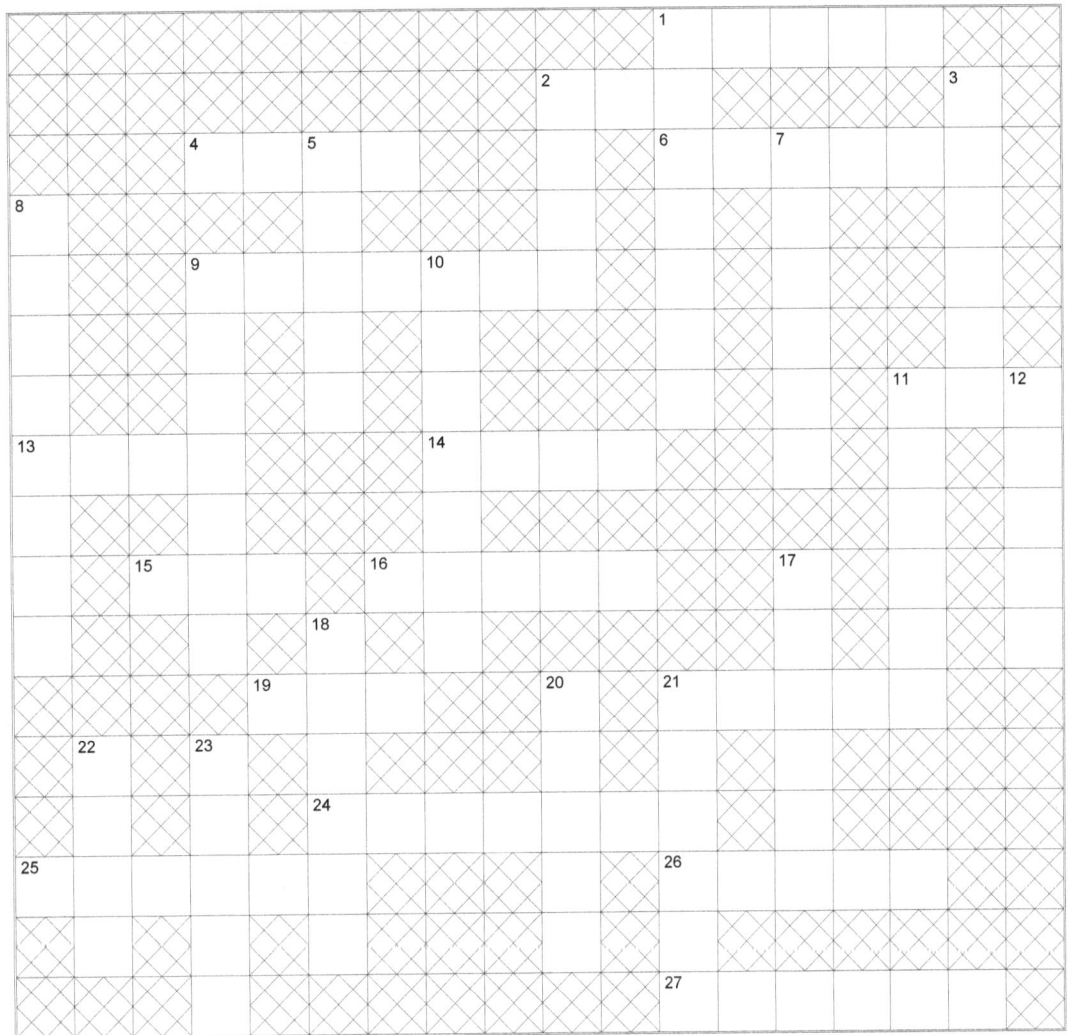

Across
1. Looked like a Saint Bernard puppy
2. Bryon did this a lot, according to Charlie
4. Invited Bryon to their parties
6. The kids drove up and down here
9. M&M and Cathy's last name
11. Bryon was given Charlie's
13. Reason for Bryon's beating by the Shephards
14. Dirty ___ had brass knuckles
15. Leader of the Shepherd gang
16. M&M's hippie nickname: Baby ___
19. Mark's hippie nickname
21. An innocent chick
24. Bryon's pool talent
25. Told her friends to kill Mike
26. Short; round; a real nut: ___ Jones
27. Mark thought Mike was ___

Down
1. Bryon thought he resembled one: St. ___
2. Mark resembled one
3. Mark cut her hair to get even for the fight
5. Tried to jump M&M
7. Weapon used on Mark's head
8. Angela and Curly's last name
9. Saved Mark's and Bryon's lives
10. M&M saw them on his bad trip
11. Mark's real father
12. Van-driving hippie college student
17. Bryon's was in the hospital
18. M&M's criticized his hair and grades
20. Mark was selling them
21. Unknowing object of Angela's affections
22. Bryon's game
23. Bryon and Cathy's first date

That Was Then, This Is Now Crossword 1 Answer Key

Across
1. Looked like a Saint Bernard puppy
2. Bryon did this a lot, according to Charlie
4. Invited Bryon to their parties
6. The kids drove up and down here
9. M&M and Cathy's last name
11. Bryon was given Charlie's
13. Reason for Bryon's beating by the Shephards
14. Dirty ___ had brass knuckles
15. Leader of the Shepherd gang
16. M&M's hippie nickname: Baby ___
19. Mark's hippie nickname
21. An innocent chick
24. Bryon's pool talent
25. Told her friends to kill Mike
26. Short; round; a real nut: ___ Jones
27. Mark thought Mike was ___

Down
1. Bryon thought he resembled one: St. ___
2. Mark resembled one
3. Mark cut her hair to get even for the fight
5. Tried to jump M&M
7. Weapon used on Mark's head
8. Angela and Curly's last name
9. Saved Mark's and Bryon's lives
10. M&M saw them on his bad trip
11. Mark's real father
12. Van-driving hippie college student
17. Bryon's was in the hospital
18. M&M's criticized his hair and grades
20. Mark was selling them
21. Unknowing object of Angela's affections
22. Bryon's game
23. Bryon and Cathy's first date

That Was Then, This Is Now Crossword 2

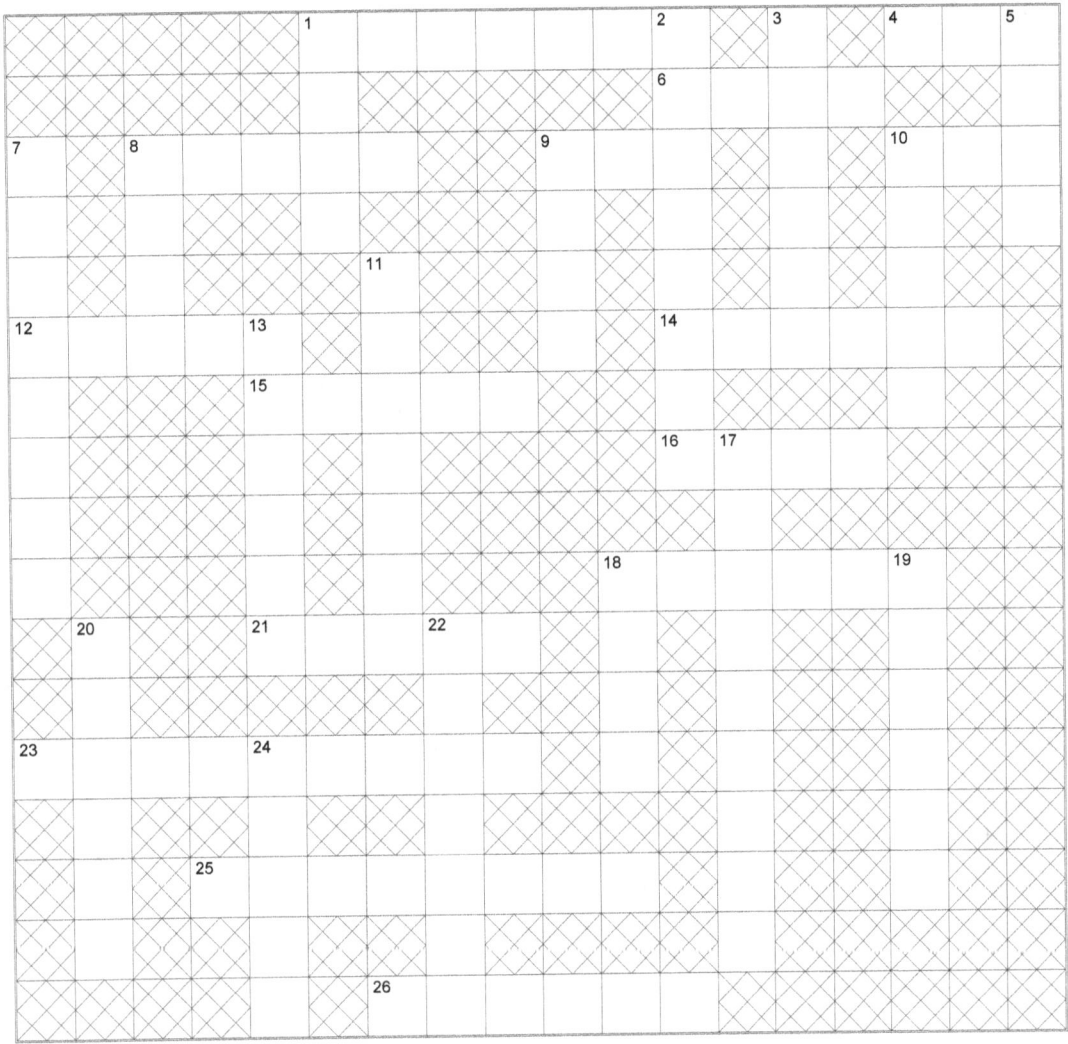

Across
1. M&M saw them on his bad trip
4. Leader of the Shepherd gang
6. Reason for Bryon's beating by the Shephards
8. M&M wore this medallion
9. Bryon did this a lot, according to Charlie
10. Bryon was given Charlie's
12. Mark was selling them
14. Mark cut her hair to get even for the fight
15. Short; round; a real nut: ___ Jones
16. Dirty ___ had brass knuckles
18. Bryon's was in the hospital
21. Bryon and Cathy's first date
23. Mark borrowed his car
25. It was the same as buying, according to Mark
26. Wanted to get even with Bryon and Mark

Down
1. Invited Bryon to their parties
2. Angela and Curly's last name
3. Mark's car talent: Hot-___
5. He looked like a friendly lion
7. Bryon's mother was here for a while
8. Bryon's game
9. Mark resembled one
10. Tried to jump M&M
11. M&M and Cathy's last name
13. Mark thought Mike was ___
17. Bryon had never been able to accept it
18. He was beaten for defending a black girl
19. The kids drove up and down here
20. Unknowing object of Angela's affections
22. Saved Mark's and Bryon's lives
24. An innocent chick

That Was Then, This Is Now Crossword 2 Answer Key

						1 S	P	I	D	E	R	2 S		3 W		4 T	I	5 M
						O						6 H	A	I	R			A
7 H		8 P	E	A	C	E			9 L	I	E			R		10 C	A	R
O		O				S			I		P			I		U		K
S		O						11 C			O			N		R		
12 P	I	L	L	S		13 S		A			N		14 A	N	G	E	L	A
I				15 T	E	R	R	Y			R					Y		
T				U		L					16 D	17 A	V	E				
A				P		S						U						
L				I		O			18 M	O	T	H	E	19 R				
	20 C			21 D	A	N	22 C	E				H		I				
	U						H					O		B				
23 P	R	I	N	24 C	I	P	A	L				R		B				
	T			A			R					I		O				
	I		25 S	T	E	A	L	I	N	G		T		N				
	S			H			I					Y						
				Y		26 T	E	X	A	N	S							

Across
1. M&M saw them on his bad trip
4. Leader of the Shepherd gang
6. Reason for Bryon's beating by the Shephards
8. M&M wore this medallion
9. Bryon did this a lot, according to Charlie
10. Bryon was given Charlie's
12. Mark was selling them
14. Mark cut her hair to get even for the fight
15. Short; round; a real nut: ___ Jones
16. Dirty ___ had brass knuckles
18. Bryon's was in the hospital
21. Bryon and Cathy's first date
23. Mark borrowed his car
25. It was the same as buying, according to Mark
26. Wanted to get even with Bryon and Mark

Down
1. Invited Bryon to their parties
2. Angela and Curly's last name
3. Mark's car talent: Hot-___
5. He looked like a friendly lion
7. Bryon's mother was here for a while
8. Bryon's game
9. Mark resembled one
10. Tried to jump M&M
11. M&M and Cathy's last name
13. Mark thought Mike was ___
17. Bryon had never been able to accept it
18. He was beaten for defending a black girl
19. The kids drove up and down here
20. Unknowing object of Angela's affections
22. Saved Mark's and Bryon's lives
24. An innocent chick

That Was Then, This Is Now Crossword 3

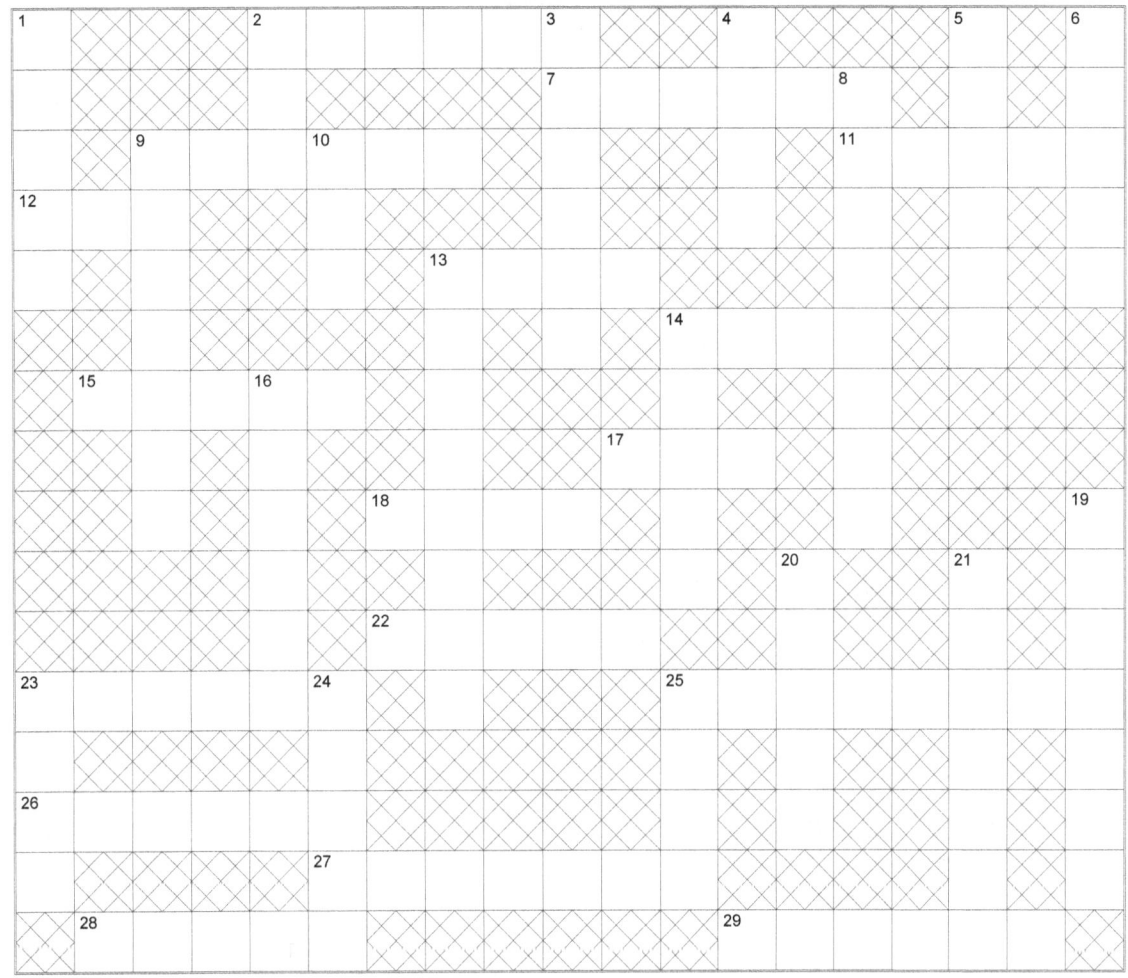

Across
2. Unknowing object of Angela's affections
7. Wanted to get even with Bryon and Mark
9. Weapon used on Mark's head
11. Short; round; a real nut: ___ Jones
12. Bryon did this a lot, according to Charlie
13. Reason for Bryon's beating by the Shephards
14. Bryon's game
15. Bryon and Cathy's first date
17. Bryon was given Charlie's
18. He was beaten for defending a black girl
22. An innocent chick
23. Bryon's was in the hospital
25. Angela and Curly's last name
26. The kids drove up and down here
27. Bryon's last name
28. Tried to jump M&M
29. M&M's criticized his hair and grades

Down
1. Mark was selling them
2. Mark's hippie nickname
3. Mark thought Mike was ___
4. Dirty ___ had brass knuckles
5. Mark's car talent: Hot-___
6. Looked like a Saint Bernard puppy
8. It was the same as buying, according to Mark
9. Bryon thought he resembled one: St. ___
10. Leader of the Shepherd gang
13. Bryon's mother was here for a while
14. M&M wore this medallion
16. Told her friends to kill Mike
19. M&M saw them on his bad trip
20. M&M's hippie nickname: Baby ___
21. Saved Mark's and Bryon's lives
23. He looked like a friendly lion
24. Van-driving hippie college student
25. Invited Bryon to their parties

That Was Then, This Is Now Crossword 3 Answer Key

Across
2. Unknowing object of Angela's affections
7. Wanted to get even with Bryon and Mark
9. Weapon used on Mark's head
11. Short; round; a real nut: ___ Jones
12. Bryon did this a lot, according to Charlie
13. Reason for Bryon's beating by the Shephards
14. Bryon's game
15. Bryon and Cathy's first date
17. Bryon was given Charlie's
18. He was beaten for defending a black girl
22. An innocent chick
23. Bryon's was in the hospital
25. Angela and Curly's last name
26. The kids drove up and down here
27. Bryon's last name
28. Tried to jump M&M
29. M&M's criticized his hair and grades

Down
1. Mark was selling them
2. Mark's hippie nickname
3. Mark thought Mike was ___
4. Dirty ___ had brass knuckles
5. Mark's car talent: Hot-___
6. Looked like a Saint Bernard puppy
8. It was the same as buying, according to Mark
9. Bryon thought he resembled one: St. ___
10. Leader of the Shepherd gang
13. Bryon's mother was here for a while
14. M&M wore this medallion
16. Told her friends to kill Mike
19. M&M saw them on his bad trip
20. M&M's hippie nickname: Baby ___
21. Saved Mark's and Bryon's lives
23. He looked like a friendly lion
24. Van-driving hippie college student
25. Invited Bryon to their parties

That Was Then, This Is Now Crossword 4

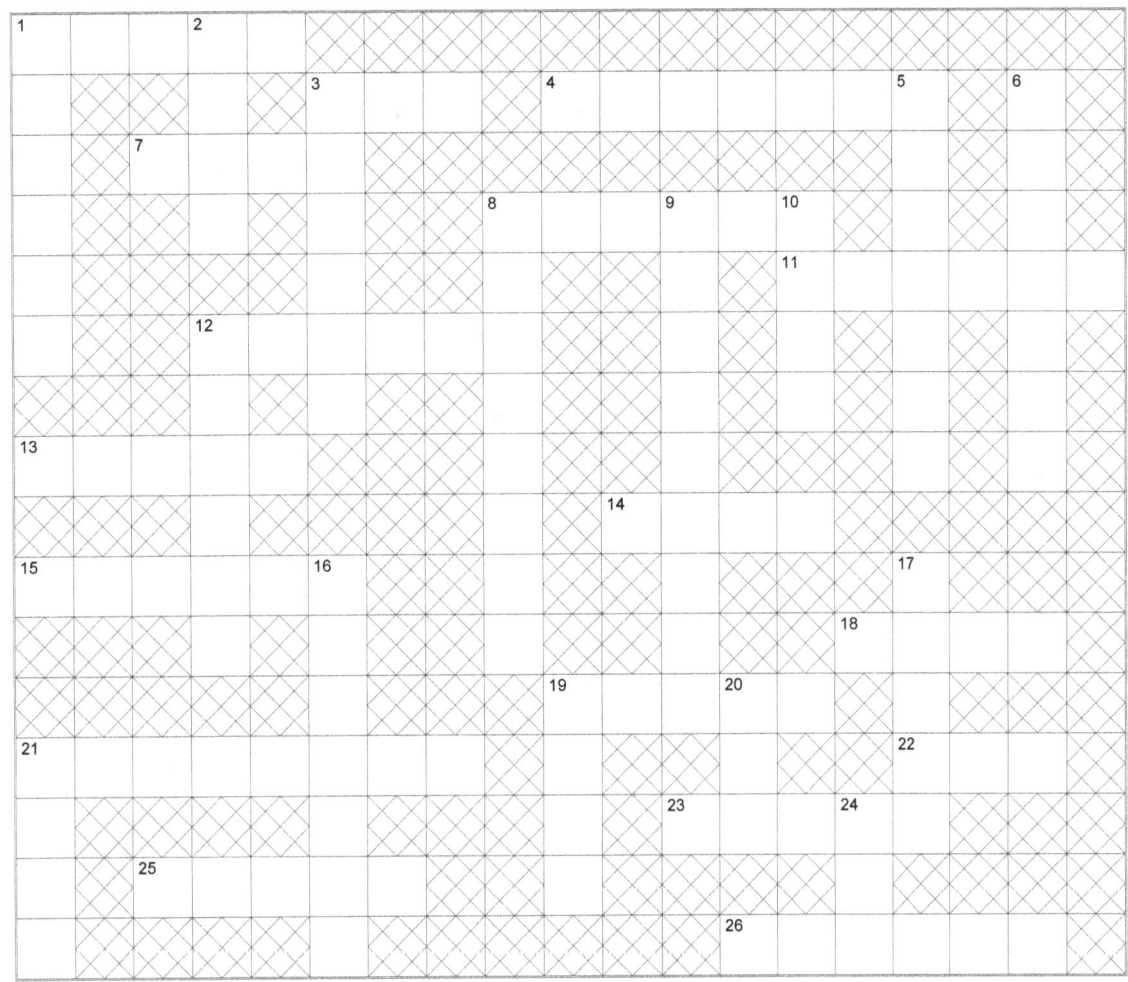

Across
1. An innocent chick
3. Leader of the Shepherd gang
4. Bryon thought he resembled one: St. ___
7. He was beaten for defending a black girl
8. Mark thought Mike was ___
11. Mark cut her hair to get even for the fight
12. Told her friends to kill Mike
13. Short; round; a real nut: ___ Jones
14. Mark resembled one
15. Mark's car talent: Hot-___
18. He looked like a friendly lion
19. Mark was selling them
21. Angela and Curly's last name
22. Bryon was given Charlie's
23. M&M wore this medallion
25. M&M's hippie nickname: Baby ___
26. Weapon used on Mark's head

Down
1. Mark's real father
2. Reason for Bryon's beating by the Shephards
3. Wanted to get even with Bryon and Mark
5. Bryon's last name
6. M&M and Cathy's last name
8. It was the same as buying, according to Mark
9. Mark borrowed his car
10. Dirty ___ had brass knuckles
12. Unknowing object of Angela's affections
16. Mike described himself this way: Sir ___
17. Bryon and Cathy's first date
19. Bryon's game
20. Bryon did this a lot, according to Charlie
21. Invited Bryon to their parties
24. Mark's hippie nickname

That Was Then, This Is Now Crossword 4 Answer Key

	1 C	A	T	2 H	Y								
	O			A		3 T	I	M	4 B	E	R	N	A	R	5 D		6 C
	W		7 M	I	K	E									O		A
	B		R			X		8 S	T	U	9 P	I	10 D			U		R
	O					A		T			R		11 A	N	G	E	L	A
	Y		12 C	O	N	N	I	E			I		V			L		S
			U		S			A			N		E			A		O
	13 T	E	R	R	Y			L			C					S		N
			T					I		14 L	I	O	N				
	15 W	I	R	I	16 G			N			P					17 D	
			S		A			G			A				18 M	A	R	K
					L				19 P	I	20 L	L	S			N		
	21 S	H	E	P	H	A	R	D		O		I				22 C	A	R
	O				H					O		23 P	E	24 A	C	E	
	C		25 F	R	E	A	K			L				A		
	S				D						26 B	O	T	T	L	E

Across
1. An innocent chick
3. Leader of the Shepherd gang
4. Bryon thought he resembled one: St. ___
7. He was beaten for defending a black girl
8. Mark thought Mike was ___
11. Mark cut her hair to get even for the fight
12. Told her friends to kill Mike
13. Short; round; a real nut: ___ Jones
14. Mark resembled one
15. Mark's car talent: Hot-___
18. He looked like a friendly lion
19. Mark was selling them
21. Angela and Curly's last name
22. Bryon was given Charlie's
23. M&M wore this medallion
25. M&M's hippie nickname: Baby ___
26. Weapon used on Mark's head

Down
1. Mark's real father
2. Reason for Bryon's beating by the Shephards
3. Wanted to get even with Bryon and Mark
5. Bryon's last name
6. M&M and Cathy's last name
8. It was the same as buying, according to Mark
9. Mark borrowed his car
10. Dirty ___ had brass knuckles
12. Unknowing object of Angela's affections
16. Mike described himself this way: Sir ___
17. Bryon and Cathy's first date
19. Bryon's game
20. Bryon did this a lot, according to Charlie
21. Invited Bryon to their parties
24. Mark's hippie nickname

That Was Then, This Is Now

CONNIE	PRINCIPAL	CHARLIE	SOCS	BOTTLE
PILLS	BRYON	PEACE	CAR	CAT
BERNARD	CATHY	FREE SPACE	STUPID	CARLSON
ANGELA	SHEPHARD	CORVETTE	HUSTLER	FATHER
SHOTGUN	MIKE	AUTHORITY	SPIDERS	RANDY

That Was Then, This Is Now

TEXANS	TERRY	POOL	RIBBON	GALAHAD
CURLY	DAVE	DANCE	HOSPITAL	FREAK
LIE	COWBOY	FREE SPACE	TIM	WIRING
MOTHER	STEALING	CURTIS	DOUGLAS	HAIR
RANDY	SPIDERS	AUTHORITY	MIKE	SHOTGUN

That Was Then, This Is Now

PEACE	POOL	HUSTLER	CATHY	SHOTGUN
BRYON	CURTIS	BOTTLE	PRINCIPAL	TERRY
LIE	DAVE	FREE SPACE	FATHER	DANCE
CAT	CONNIE	TIM	CHARLIE	SPIDERS
RIBBON	PILLS	CAR	MOTHER	MIKE

That Was Then, This Is Now

HAIR	STEALING	CORVETTE	AUTHORITY	STUPID
ANGELA	WIRING	CURLY	RANDY	COWBOY
GALAHAD	HOSPITAL	FREE SPACE	SHEPHARD	TEXANS
CARLSON	FREAK	MARK	DOUGLAS	BERNARD
MIKE	MOTHER	CAR	PILLS	RIBBON

That Was Then, This Is Now

MOTHER	SHOTGUN	DAVE	BERNARD	RANDY
TIM	FATHER	CORVETTE	RIBBON	TEXANS
HUSTLER	CATHY	FREE SPACE	MIKE	CHARLIE
GALAHAD	CONNIE	CAR	CAT	BOTTLE
FREAK	DANCE	TERRY	CURLY	HOSPITAL

That Was Then, This Is Now

STEALING	PRINCIPAL	LIE	MARK	PILLS
ANGELA	DOUGLAS	CARLSON	PEACE	STUPID
CURTIS	SOCS	FREE SPACE	COWBOY	SHEPHARD
LION	POOL	WIRING	HAIR	SPIDERS
HOSPITAL	CURLY	TERRY	DANCE	FREAK

That Was Then, This Is Now

MIKE	PEACE	ANGELA	SPIDERS	CARLSON
FREAK	TERRY	DAVE	PILLS	DANCE
CHARLIE	STUPID	FREE SPACE	SHEPHARD	CORVETTE
CURLY	DOUGLAS	STEALING	BOTTLE	COWBOY
LION	BERNARD	LIE	RANDY	POOL

That Was Then, This Is Now

CONNIE	HUSTLER	HOSPITAL	CAR	CURTIS
GALAHAD	TEXANS	SHOTGUN	BRYON	RIBBON
AUTHORITY	MARK	FREE SPACE	FATHER	MOTHER
PRINCIPAL	WIRING	SOCS	CATHY	TIM
POOL	RANDY	LIE	BERNARD	LION

That Was Then, This Is Now

CURLY	RIBBON	CAR	CATHY	CURTIS
DAVE	COWBOY	SHEPHARD	FATHER	MARK
FREAK	ANGELA	FREE SPACE	CORVETTE	WIRING
PEACE	MOTHER	TIM	TERRY	SHOTGUN
DANCE	SOCS	AUTHORITY	CARLSON	TEXANS

That Was Then, This Is Now

SPIDERS	MIKE	PILLS	CONNIE	HOSPITAL
PRINCIPAL	RANDY	CAT	HAIR	HUSTLER
LIE	BERNARD	FREE SPACE	LION	POOL
BRYON	CHARLIE	STEALING	DOUGLAS	GALAHAD
TEXANS	CARLSON	AUTHORITY	SOCS	DANCE

That Was Then, This Is Now

CAR	TIM	MIKE	MOTHER	BRYON
FATHER	STUPID	AUTHORITY	PEACE	SHOTGUN
LIE	STEALING	FREE SPACE	CARLSON	LION
SHEPHARD	DOUGLAS	COWBOY	CURTIS	HAIR
CAT	GALAHAD	CURLY	PRINCIPAL	ANGELA

That Was Then, This Is Now

CONNIE	HUSTLER	SPIDERS	RANDY	TERRY
BERNARD	TEXANS	HOSPITAL	POOL	PILLS
MARK	CATHY	FREE SPACE	CORVETTE	BOTTLE
RIBBON	CHARLIE	SOCS	FREAK	DAVE
ANGELA	PRINCIPAL	CURLY	GALAHAD	CAT

That Was Then, This Is Now

RANDY	FREAK	LIE	PEACE	SHEPHARD
FATHER	GALAHAD	MARK	CARLSON	DOUGLAS
POOL	SPIDERS	FREE SPACE	STEALING	PRINCIPAL
SHOTGUN	CAT	BOTTLE	HAIR	PILLS
TERRY	HUSTLER	CATHY	COWBOY	RIBBON

That Was Then, This Is Now

MIKE	LION	TIM	BRYON	STUPID
DANCE	WIRING	CONNIE	HOSPITAL	CURTIS
CHARLIE	SOCS	FREE SPACE	ANGELA	CAR
AUTHORITY	CURLY	MOTHER	DAVE	CORVETTE
RIBBON	COWBOY	CATHY	HUSTLER	TERRY

That Was Then, This Is Now

POOL	CATHY	RIBBON	BERNARD	LIE
PILLS	STEALING	FREAK	SPIDERS	DOUGLAS
TIM	CAR	FREE SPACE	SHOTGUN	MIKE
CARLSON	DANCE	LION	ANGELA	PRINCIPAL
MARK	CURLY	MOTHER	CHARLIE	SHEPHARD

That Was Then, This Is Now

HUSTLER	CAT	RANDY	CONNIE	PEACE
TEXANS	WIRING	HAIR	SOCS	CORVETTE
HOSPITAL	AUTHORITY	FREE SPACE	GALAHAD	BRYON
CURTIS	STUPID	BOTTLE	TERRY	FATHER
SHEPHARD	CHARLIE	MOTHER	CURLY	MARK

That Was Then, This Is Now

RIBBON	LION	MARK	CHARLIE	TIM
PILLS	DAVE	STUPID	PRINCIPAL	CORVETTE
MOTHER	HUSTLER	FREE SPACE	MIKE	BRYON
HAIR	POOL	CATHY	PEACE	SHEPHARD
SPIDERS	RANDY	TEXANS	AUTHORITY	SHOTGUN

That Was Then, This Is Now

TERRY	LIE	CONNIE	CURLY	BOTTLE
DANCE	DOUGLAS	HOSPITAL	COWBOY	WIRING
ANGELA	STEALING	FREE SPACE	GALAHAD	BERNARD
CURTIS	SOCS	FREAK	CARLSON	CAT
SHOTGUN	AUTHORITY	TEXANS	RANDY	SPIDERS

That Was Then, This Is Now

CATHY	CURLY	SHOTGUN	CARLSON	RIBBON
BOTTLE	STUPID	CHARLIE	FREAK	PEACE
DAVE	RANDY	FREE SPACE	POOL	BERNARD
DOUGLAS	ANGELA	CONNIE	CORVETTE	TIM
PILLS	SHEPHARD	CURTIS	CAR	GALAHAD

That Was Then, This Is Now

TEXANS	WIRING	HAIR	FATHER	HOSPITAL
LIE	PRINCIPAL	AUTHORITY	CAT	HUSTLER
SOCS	DANCE	FREE SPACE	COWBOY	TERRY
LION	MIKE	MARK	BRYON	STEALING
GALAHAD	CAR	CURTIS	SHEPHARD	PILLS

That Was Then, This Is Now

HUSTLER	COWBOY	GALAHAD	DAVE	MIKE
SOCS	DANCE	TIM	CHARLIE	SHOTGUN
CARLSON	TEXANS	FREE SPACE	LIE	CURLY
PILLS	CATHY	WIRING	BOTTLE	STEALING
MOTHER	POOL	LION	BERNARD	STUPID

That Was Then, This Is Now

TERRY	DOUGLAS	CONNIE	FREAK	PRINCIPAL
CAR	PEACE	AUTHORITY	FATHER	CURTIS
MARK	RANDY	FREE SPACE	BRYON	CORVETTE
SHEPHARD	RIBBON	SPIDERS	ANGELA	HAIR
STUPID	BERNARD	LION	POOL	MOTHER

That Was Then, This Is Now

DANCE	HUSTLER	STEALING	POOL	SOCS
LION	PRINCIPAL	SHOTGUN	MIKE	ANGELA
HAIR	CARLSON	FREE SPACE	TIM	GALAHAD
SHEPHARD	PILLS	AUTHORITY	FREAK	BERNARD
COWBOY	HOSPITAL	DOUGLAS	WIRING	CAR

That Was Then, This Is Now

LIE	PEACE	CORVETTE	RANDY	CAT
SPIDERS	MOTHER	BOTTLE	CATHY	RIBBON
BRYON	DAVE	FREE SPACE	CURLY	CONNIE
CURTIS	CHARLIE	MARK	STUPID	TEXANS
CAR	WIRING	DOUGLAS	HOSPITAL	COWBOY

That Was Then, This Is Now

CURLY	TEXANS	PILLS	RANDY	CAT
HAIR	DOUGLAS	PEACE	LION	LIE
BOTTLE	STUPID	FREE SPACE	BRYON	MARK
HOSPITAL	HUSTLER	MOTHER	TERRY	CORVETTE
ANGELA	CHARLIE	STEALING	GALAHAD	WIRING

That Was Then, This Is Now

SHEPHARD	POOL	MIKE	SHOTGUN	CATHY
DANCE	FREAK	COWBOY	BERNARD	TIM
CURTIS	CAR	FREE SPACE	RIBBON	DAVE
SOCS	CONNIE	CARLSON	PRINCIPAL	FATHER
WIRING	GALAHAD	STEALING	CHARLIE	ANGELA

That Was Then, This Is Now

CORVETTE	MARK	ANGELA	TERRY	TIM
DANCE	FREAK	STUPID	BRYON	COWBOY
RANDY	HAIR	FREE SPACE	MIKE	CONNIE
HOSPITAL	SHOTGUN	HUSTLER	FATHER	WIRING
CARLSON	AUTHORITY	CAR	LION	CURTIS

That Was Then, This Is Now

SPIDERS	SHEPHARD	CHARLIE	PEACE	RIBBON
BERNARD	CURLY	MOTHER	PRINCIPAL	TEXANS
DOUGLAS	CATHY	FREE SPACE	BOTTLE	PILLS
SOCS	DAVE	POOL	GALAHAD	CAT
CURTIS	LION	CAR	AUTHORITY	CARLSON

That Was Then, This Is Now

HOSPITAL	SOCS	CHARLIE	CONNIE	HUSTLER
CAR	LIE	CURLY	DANCE	HAIR
CAT	PILLS	FREE SPACE	RANDY	MARK
MOTHER	TIM	BRYON	POOL	WIRING
AUTHORITY	TEXANS	BERNARD	COWBOY	PEACE

That Was Then, This Is Now

GALAHAD	BOTTLE	FATHER	CATHY	ANGELA
LION	CURTIS	CARLSON	SPIDERS	DOUGLAS
RIBBON	PRINCIPAL	FREE SPACE	FREAK	SHOTGUN
STEALING	TERRY	CORVETTE	SHEPHARD	MIKE
PEACE	COWBOY	BERNARD	TEXANS	AUTHORITY

That Was Then, This Is Now

FATHER	TERRY	CURLY	SHEPHARD	POOL
MARK	FREAK	HUSTLER	CONNIE	PEACE
CORVETTE	CAR	FREE SPACE	GALAHAD	CARLSON
RIBBON	STUPID	BERNARD	SHOTGUN	MOTHER
CATHY	SPIDERS	MIKE	HOSPITAL	PRINCIPAL

That Was Then, This Is Now

DANCE	STEALING	HAIR	DAVE	BRYON
PILLS	DOUGLAS	TIM	TEXANS	LIE
AUTHORITY	WIRING	FREE SPACE	LION	ANGELA
CHARLIE	SOCS	COWBOY	RANDY	CURTIS
PRINCIPAL	HOSPITAL	MIKE	SPIDERS	CATHY

That Was Then, This Is Now Vocabulary Word List

No.	Word	Clue/Definition
1.	ABRUPTLY	Suddenly
2.	AFOREMENTIONED	Said before
3.	ASSAULT	Attack
4.	COMMUNE	A group of people living together
5.	CONTORTED	Twisted out of shape
6.	DESPERATELY	Hopelessly
7.	FLOUNCED	Moved in a bouncing or lively in manner
8.	FORMALITIES	Customs
9.	GRAVELY	Seriously
10.	GULF	Distance
11.	HOSTILITY	Conflict
12.	HUB	Center
13.	HYSTERICAL	In an uncontrolled, excitable state
14.	INCLINED	Tending
15.	INCREDULOUS	Doubtful; disbelieving
16.	INTENT	Resolute
17.	IRRATIONALLY	Not logically
18.	LAME	Having an injured leg or foot
19.	LANKY	Tall and skinny
20.	MINOR	One who is under the legal age
21.	OBLIGINGLY	Willingly
22.	OBSCURE	Unclear
23.	PLEADING	Begging
24.	PROBATION	Supervised freedom for lawbreakers
25.	PROFOUND	Intellectual
26.	RELAPSE	Slipping back
27.	REMINISCING	Remembering past events
28.	SARCASTICALLY	In a mocking manner
29.	SASSY	Rude
30.	SAUNTERED	Strolled
31.	SINISTER	Threatening
32.	SLACKED	Slowed
33.	SLIGHT	Light in form or build
34.	SMIRKING	Sneering
35.	SOLE	Single; only
36.	TACTFULLY	Dealing with people in a skillful way
37.	TAUNTING	Insulting; mean teasing
38.	VAGUE	Indistinct
39.	VENGEFUL	Wanting to give punishment for a wrong
40.	WITTICISM	Joke

That Was Then, This Is Now Vocabulary Fill In The Blanks 1

_____ 1. Indistinct

_____ 2. Seriously

_____ 3. Threatening

_____ 4. In a mocking manner

_____ 5. Supervised freedom for lawbreakers

_____ 6. Slipping back

_____ 7. Doubtful; disbelieving

_____ 8. Unclear

_____ 9. Having an injured leg or foot

_____ 10. Strolled

_____ 11. Dealing with people in a skillful way

_____ 12. Distance

_____ 13. In an uncontrolled, excitable state

_____ 14. Moved in a bouncing or lively in manner

_____ 15. Tending

_____ 16. Light in form or build

_____ 17. Rude

_____ 18. Remembering past events

_____ 19. Begging

_____ 20. Slowed

That Was Then, This Is Now Vocabulary Fill In The Blanks 1 Answer Key

VAGUE	1. Indistinct
GRAVELY	2. Seriously
SINISTER	3. Threatening
SARCASTICALLY	4. In a mocking manner
PROBATION	5. Supervised freedom for lawbreakers
RELAPSE	6. Slipping back
INCREDULOUS	7. Doubtful; disbelieving
OBSCURE	8. Unclear
LAME	9. Having an injured leg or foot
SAUNTERED	10. Strolled
TACTFULLY	11. Dealing with people in a skillful way
GULF	12. Distance
HYSTERICAL	13. In an uncontrolled, excitable state
FLOUNCED	14. Moved in a bouncing or lively in manner
INCLINED	15. Tending
SLIGHT	16. Light in form or build
SASSY	17. Rude
REMINISCING	18. Remembering past events
PLEADING	19. Begging
SLACKED	20. Slowed

That Was Then, This Is Now Vocabulary Fill In The Blanks 2

_____ 1. Remembering past events
_____ 2. Unclear
_____ 3. Slipping back
_____ 4. Having an injured leg or foot
_____ 5. Strolled
_____ 6. Twisted out of shape
_____ 7. Tall and skinny
_____ 8. Distance
_____ 9. In a mocking manner
_____ 10. Intellectual
_____ 11. Light in form or build
_____ 12. Conflict
_____ 13. Seriously
_____ 14. Customs
_____ 15. Dealing with people in a skillful way
_____ 16. Not logically
_____ 17. Begging
_____ 18. Tending
_____ 19. A group of people living together
_____ 20. Threatening

That Was Then, This Is Now Vocabulary Fill In The Blanks 2 Answer Key

REMINISCING	1.	Remembering past events
OBSCURE	2.	Unclear
RELAPSE	3.	Slipping back
LAME	4.	Having an injured leg or foot
SAUNTERED	5.	Strolled
CONTORTED	6.	Twisted out of shape
LANKY	7.	Tall and skinny
GULF	8.	Distance
SARCASTICALLY	9.	In a mocking manner
PROFOUND	10.	Intellectual
SLIGHT	11.	Light in form or build
HOSTILITY	12.	Conflict
GRAVELY	13.	Seriously
FORMALITIES	14.	Customs
TACTFULLY	15.	Dealing with people in a skillful way
IRRATIONALLY	16.	Not logically
PLEADING	17.	Begging
INCLINED	18.	Tending
COMMUNE	19.	A group of people living together
SINISTER	20.	Threatening

That Was Then, This Is Now Vocabulary Fill In The Blanks 3

_____ 1. A group of people living together

_____ 2. Attack

_____ 3. Hopelessly

_____ 4. Sneering

_____ 5. Said before

_____ 6. Conflict

_____ 7. Insulting; mean teasing

_____ 8. Suddenly

_____ 9. Distance

_____ 10. Center

_____ 11. Slowed

_____ 12. Intellectual

_____ 13. Rude

_____ 14. In a mocking manner

_____ 15. Not logically

_____ 16. Tall and skinny

_____ 17. Willingly

_____ 18. Moved in a bouncing or lively in manner

_____ 19. Slipping back

_____ 20. Wanting to give punishment for a wrong

That Was Then, This Is Now Vocabulary Fill In The Blanks 3 Answer Key

COMMUNE	1. A group of people living together
ASSAULT	2. Attack
DESPERATELY	3. Hopelessly
SMIRKING	4. Sneering
AFOREMENTIONED	5. Said before
HOSTILITY	6. Conflict
TAUNTING	7. Insulting; mean teasing
ABRUPTLY	8. Suddenly
GULF	9. Distance
HUB	10. Center
SLACKED	11. Slowed
PROFOUND	12. Intellectual
SASSY	13. Rude
SARCASTICALLY	14. In a mocking manner
IRRATIONALLY	15. Not logically
LANKY	16. Tall and skinny
OBLIGINGLY	17. Willingly
FLOUNCED	18. Moved in a bouncing or lively in manner
RELAPSE	19. Slipping back
VENGEFUL	20. Wanting to give punishment for a wrong

That Was Then, This Is Now Vocabulary Fill In The Blanks 4

_____   1. In an uncontrolled, excitable state
_____   2. Resolute
_____   3. Twisted out of shape
_____   4. Conflict
_____   5. Doubtful; disbelieving
_____   6. Tall and skinny
_____   7. Willingly
_____   8. Attack
_____   9. Center
_____   10. Threatening
_____   11. Distance
_____   12. Sneering
_____   13. Said before
_____   14. Joke
_____   15. Remembering past events
_____   16. Suddenly
_____   17. Intellectual
_____   18. Strolled
_____   19. Slipping back
_____   20. Light in form or build

That Was Then, This Is Now Vocabulary Fill In The Blanks 4 Answer Key

HYSTERICAL	1. In an uncontrolled, excitable state
INTENT	2. Resolute
CONTORTED	3. Twisted out of shape
HOSTILITY	4. Conflict
INCREDULOUS	5. Doubtful; disbelieving
LANKY	6. Tall and skinny
OBLIGINGLY	7. Willingly
ASSAULT	8. Attack
HUB	9. Center
SINISTER	10. Threatening
GULF	11. Distance
SMIRKING	12. Sneering
AFOREMENTIONED	13. Said before
WITTICISM	14. Joke
REMINISCING	15. Remembering past events
ABRUPTLY	16. Suddenly
PROFOUND	17. Intellectual
SAUNTERED	18. Strolled
RELAPSE	19. Slipping back
SLIGHT	20. Light in form or build

That Was Then, This Is Now Vocabulary Matching 1

___ 1. LANKY   A. Customs
___ 2. SAUNTERED   B. Center
___ 3. SLIGHT   C. Sneering
___ 4. GULF   D. Indistinct
___ 5. TAUNTING   E. In an uncontrolled, excitable state
___ 6. SARCASTICALLY   F. Single; only
___ 7. FLOUNCED   G. Doubtful; disbelieving
___ 8. GRAVELY   H. Insulting; mean teasing
___ 9. REMINISCING   I. Light in form or build
___10. SMIRKING   J. Tall and skinny
___11. IRRATIONALLY   K. In a mocking manner
___12. CONTORTED   L. Distance
___13. FORMALITIES   M. Moved in a bouncing or lively in manner
___14. OBLIGINGLY   N. Hopelessly
___15. WITTICISM   O. Remembering past events
___16. SOLE   P. Joke
___17. PROFOUND   Q. Wanting to give punishment for a wrong
___18. OBSCURE   R. Strolled
___19. HUB   S. Twisted out of shape
___20. HYSTERICAL   T. Willingly
___21. DESPERATELY   U. Not logically
___22. VAGUE   V. Seriously
___23. HOSTILITY   W. Intellectual
___24. VENGEFUL   X. Unclear
___25. INCREDULOUS   Y. Conflict

That Was Then, This Is Now Vocabulary Matching 1 Answer Key

J - 1. LANKY	A.	Customs
R - 2. SAUNTERED	B.	Center
I - 3. SLIGHT	C.	Sneering
L - 4. GULF	D.	Indistinct
H - 5. TAUNTING	E.	In an uncontrolled, excitable state
K - 6. SARCASTICALLY	F.	Single; only
M - 7. FLOUNCED	G.	Doubtful; disbelieving
V - 8. GRAVELY	H.	Insulting; mean teasing
O - 9. REMINISCING	I.	Light in form or build
C - 10. SMIRKING	J.	Tall and skinny
U - 11. IRRATIONALLY	K.	In a mocking manner
S - 12. CONTORTED	L.	Distance
A - 13. FORMALITIES	M.	Moved in a bouncing or lively in manner
T - 14. OBLIGINGLY	N.	Hopelessly
P - 15. WITTICISM	O.	Remembering past events
F - 16. SOLE	P.	Joke
W - 17. PROFOUND	Q.	Wanting to give punishment for a wrong
X - 18. OBSCURE	R.	Strolled
B - 19. HUB	S.	Twisted out of shape
E - 20. HYSTERICAL	T.	Willingly
N - 21. DESPERATELY	U.	Not logically
D - 22. VAGUE	V.	Seriously
Y - 23. HOSTILITY	W.	Intellectual
Q - 24. VENGEFUL	X.	Unclear
G - 25. INCREDULOUS	Y.	Conflict

That Was Then, This Is Now Vocabulary Matching 2

___ 1. REMINISCING   A. Wanting to give punishment for a wrong
___ 2. FLOUNCED   B. Tending
___ 3. MINOR   C. Hopelessly
___ 4. AFOREMENTIONED   D. Sneering
___ 5. HUB   E. Said before
___ 6. OBSCURE   F. One who is under the legal age
___ 7. SMIRKING   G. Willingly
___ 8. LANKY   H. In a mocking manner
___ 9. VENGEFUL   I. Begging
___10. PLEADING   J. Attack
___11. TACTFULLY   K. Distance
___12. SASSY   L. Indistinct
___13. OBLIGINGLY   M. Single; only
___14. RELAPSE   N. Conflict
___15. SAUNTERED   O. Center
___16. SOLE   P. Dealing with people in a skillful way
___17. INCLINED   Q. Rude
___18. WITTICISM   R. Tall and skinny
___19. VAGUE   S. Joke
___20. SARCASTICALLY   T. Unclear
___21. GULF   U. Slipping back
___22. IRRATIONALLY   V. Moved in a bouncing or lively in manner
___23. DESPERATELY   W. Not logically
___24. ASSAULT   X. Remembering past events
___25. HOSTILITY   Y. Strolled

That Was Then, This Is Now Vocabulary Matching 2 Answer Key

X - 1. REMINISCING   A. Wanting to give punishment for a wrong
V - 2. FLOUNCED   B. Tending
F - 3. MINOR   C. Hopelessly
E - 4. AFOREMENTIONED   D. Sneering
O - 5. HUB   E. Said before
T - 6. OBSCURE   F. One who is under the legal age
D - 7. SMIRKING   G. Willingly
R - 8. LANKY   H. In a mocking manner
A - 9. VENGEFUL   I. Begging
I - 10. PLEADING   J. Attack
P - 11. TACTFULLY   K. Distance
Q - 12. SASSY   L. Indistinct
G - 13. OBLIGINGLY   M. Single; only
U - 14. RELAPSE   N. Conflict
Y - 15. SAUNTERED   O. Center
M - 16. SOLE   P. Dealing with people in a skillful way
B - 17. INCLINED   Q. Rude
S - 18. WITTICISM   R. Tall and skinny
L - 19. VAGUE   S. Joke
H - 20. SARCASTICALLY   T. Unclear
K - 21. GULF   U. Slipping back
W - 22. IRRATIONALLY   V. Moved in a bouncing or lively in manner
C - 23. DESPERATELY   W. Not logically
J - 24. ASSAULT   X. Remembering past events
N - 25. HOSTILITY   Y. Strolled

That Was Then, This Is Now Vocabulary Matching 3

___ 1. AFOREMENTIONED A. Conflict
___ 2. TAUNTING B. Said before
___ 3. FLOUNCED C. Tall and skinny
___ 4. VENGEFUL D. Strolled
___ 5. ABRUPTLY E. Indistinct
___ 6. GULF F. Begging
___ 7. INTENT G. Having an injured leg or foot
___ 8. PROFOUND H. Suddenly
___ 9. HOSTILITY I. Moved in a bouncing or lively in manner
___10. VAGUE J. Joke
___11. OBSCURE K. Supervised freedom for lawbreakers
___12. WITTICISM L. Light in form or build
___13. HUB M. Unclear
___14. PROBATION N. Slipping back
___15. SASSY O. Intellectual
___16. SLIGHT P. Insulting; mean teasing
___17. PLEADING Q. Wanting to give punishment for a wrong
___18. RELAPSE R. Customs
___19. SLACKED S. Rude
___20. SAUNTERED T. Remembering past events
___21. LAME U. Resolute
___22. LANKY V. Distance
___23. REMINISCING W. Center
___24. FORMALITIES X. Twisted out of shape
___25. CONTORTED Y. Slowed

That Was Then, This Is Now Vocabulary Matching 3 Answer Key

B - 1. AFOREMENTIONED   A. Conflict
P - 2. TAUNTING   B. Said before
I - 3. FLOUNCED   C. Tall and skinny
Q - 4. VENGEFUL   D. Strolled
H - 5. ABRUPTLY   E. Indistinct
V - 6. GULF   F. Begging
U - 7. INTENT   G. Having an injured leg or foot
O - 8. PROFOUND   H. Suddenly
A - 9. HOSTILITY   I. Moved in a bouncing or lively in manner
E - 10. VAGUE   J. Joke
M - 11. OBSCURE   K. Supervised freedom for lawbreakers
J - 12. WITTICISM   L. Light in form or build
W - 13. HUB   M. Unclear
K - 14. PROBATION   N. Slipping back
S - 15. SASSY   O. Intellectual
L - 16. SLIGHT   P. Insulting; mean teasing
F - 17. PLEADING   Q. Wanting to give punishment for a wrong
N - 18. RELAPSE   R. Customs
Y - 19. SLACKED   S. Rude
D - 20. SAUNTERED   T. Remembering past events
G - 21. LAME   U. Resolute
C - 22. LANKY   V. Distance
T - 23. REMINISCING   W. Center
R - 24. FORMALITIES   X. Twisted out of shape
X - 25. CONTORTED   Y. Slowed

That Was Then, This Is Now Vocabulary Matching 4

___ 1. MINOR   A. Center
___ 2. PROBATION   B. Hopelessly
___ 3. HUB   C. Wanting to give punishment for a wrong
___ 4. RELAPSE   D. Slipping back
___ 5. REMINISCING   E. Distance
___ 6. FORMALITIES   F. Customs
___ 7. OBLIGINGLY   G. Said before
___ 8. GULF   H. Single; only
___ 9. SLIGHT   I. Light in form or build
___10. ABRUPTLY   J. Attack
___11. INCLINED   K. Supervised freedom for lawbreakers
___12. VENGEFUL   L. Twisted out of shape
___13. COMMUNE   M. Tending
___14. INCREDULOUS   N. A group of people living together
___15. ASSAULT   O. Willingly
___16. FLOUNCED   P. Seriously
___17. SOLE   Q. Conflict
___18. GRAVELY   R. Remembering past events
___19. PROFOUND   S. Intellectual
___20. LANKY   T. Doubtful; disbelieving
___21. DESPERATELY   U. One who is under the legal age
___22. AFOREMENTIONED V. Joke
___23. CONTORTED   W. Suddenly
___24. HOSTILITY   X. Moved in a bouncing or lively in manner
___25. WITTICISM   Y. Tall and skinny

That Was Then, This Is Now Vocabulary Matching 4 Answer Key

U - 1. MINOR		A. Center
K - 2. PROBATION		B. Hopelessly
A - 3. HUB		C. Wanting to give punishment for a wrong
D - 4. RELAPSE		D. Slipping back
R - 5. REMINISCING		E. Distance
F - 6. FORMALITIES		F. Customs
O - 7. OBLIGINGLY		G. Said before
E - 8. GULF		H. Single; only
I - 9. SLIGHT		I. Light in form or build
W - 10. ABRUPTLY		J. Attack
M - 11. INCLINED		K. Supervised freedom for lawbreakers
C - 12. VENGEFUL		L. Twisted out of shape
N - 13. COMMUNE		M. Tending
T - 14. INCREDULOUS		N. A group of people living together
J - 15. ASSAULT		O. Willingly
X - 16. FLOUNCED		P. Seriously
H - 17. SOLE		Q. Conflict
P - 18. GRAVELY		R. Remembering past events
S - 19. PROFOUND		S. Intellectual
Y - 20. LANKY		T. Doubtful; disbelieving
B - 21. DESPERATELY		U. One who is under the legal age
G - 22. AFOREMENTIONED		V. Joke
L - 23. CONTORTED		W. Suddenly
Q - 24. HOSTILITY		X. Moved in a bouncing or lively in manner
V - 25. WITTICISM		Y. Tall and skinny

That Was Then, This Is Now Vocabulary Magic Squares 1

Match the definition with the vocabulary word. Put your answers in the magic squares below. When your answers are correct, all columns and rows will add to the same number.

A. INCLINED
B. SLIGHT
C. REMINISCING
D. SLACKED
E. HOSTILITY
F. HYSTERICAL
G. RELAPSE
H. VAGUE
I. INTENT
J. ASSAULT
K. CONTORTED
L. SARCASTICALLY
M. LANKY
N. ABRUPTLY
O. FLOUNCED
P. INCREDULOUS

1. Indistinct
2. Tall and skinny
3. Light in form or build
4. Twisted out of shape
5. Attack
6. Remembering past events
7. Doubtful; disbelieving
8. Conflict
9. Moved in a bouncing or lively in manner
10. In an uncontrolled, excitable state
11. Resolute
12. Slowed
13. Tending
14. In a mocking manner
15. Slipping back
16. Suddenly

A=	B=	C=	D=
E=	F=	G=	H=
I=	J=	K=	L=
M=	N=	O=	P=

That Was Then, This Is Now Vocabulary Magic Squares 1 Answer Key

Match the definition with the vocabulary word. Put your answers in the magic squares below. When your answers are correct, all columns and rows will add to the same number.

A. INCLINED
B. SLIGHT
C. REMINISCING
D. SLACKED
E. HOSTILITY
F. HYSTERICAL
G. RELAPSE
H. VAGUE
I. INTENT
J. ASSAULT
K. CONTORTED
L. SARCASTICALLY
M. LANKY
N. ABRUPTLY
O. FLOUNCED
P. INCREDULOUS

1. Indistinct
2. Tall and skinny
3. Light in form or build
4. Twisted out of shape
5. Attack
6. Remembering past events
7. Doubtful; disbelieving
8. Conflict
9. Moved in a bouncing or lively in manner
10. In an uncontrolled, excitable state
11. Resolute
12. Slowed
13. Tending
14. In a mocking manner
15. Slipping back
16. Suddenly

A=13	B=3	C=6	D=12
E=8	F=10	G=15	H=1
I=11	J=5	K=4	L=14
M=2	N=16	O=9	P=7

That Was Then, This Is Now Vocabulary Magic Squares 2

Match the definition with the vocabulary word. Put your answers in the magic squares below. When your answers are correct, all columns and rows will add to the same number.

A. INCREDULOUS
B. INCLINED
C. PROFOUND
D. VAGUE
E. REMINISCING
F. HOSTILITY
G. SINISTER
H. LANKY
I. PLEADING
J. RELAPSE
K. FORMALITIES
L. HYSTERICAL
M. FLOUNCED
N. GULF
O. AFOREMENTIONED
P. MINOR

1. Said before
2. Indistinct
3. Slipping back
4. Remembering past events
5. Begging
6. Conflict
7. One who is under the legal age
8. Intellectual
9. Tall and skinny
10. Customs
11. Doubtful; disbelieving
12. Distance
13. Tending
14. Moved in a bouncing or lively in manner
15. Threatening
16. In an uncontrolled, excitable state

A=	B=	C=	D=
E=	F=	G=	H=
I=	J=	K=	L=
M=	N=	O=	P=

That Was Then, This Is Now Vocabulary Magic Squares 2 Answer Key

Match the definition with the vocabulary word. Put your answers in the magic squares below. When your answers are correct, all columns and rows will add to the same number.

A. INCREDULOUS
B. INCLINED
C. PROFOUND
D. VAGUE
E. REMINISCING
F. HOSTILITY
G. SINISTER
H. LANKY
I. PLEADING
J. RELAPSE
K. FORMALITIES
L. HYSTERICAL
M. FLOUNCED
N. GULF
O. AFOREMENTIONED
P. MINOR

1. Said before
2. Indistinct
3. Slipping back
4. Remembering past events
5. Begging
6. Conflict
7. One who is under the legal age
8. Intellectual
9. Tall and skinny
10. Customs
11. Doubtful; disbelieving
12. Distance
13. Tending
14. Moved in a bouncing or lively in manner
15. Threatening
16. In an uncontrolled, excitable state

A=11	B=13	C=8	D=2
E=4	F=6	G=15	H=9
I=5	J=3	K=10	L=16
M=14	N=12	O=1	P=7

That Was Then, This Is Now Vocabulary Magic Squares 3

Match the definition with the vocabulary word. Put your answers in the magic squares below. When your answers are correct, all columns and rows will add to the same number.

A. SINISTER
B. RELAPSE
C. SMIRKING
D. INCREDULOUS
E. CONTORTED
F. TACTFULLY
G. SOLE
H. LAME
I. MINOR
J. HYSTERICAL
K. PLEADING
L. FORMALITIES
M. ASSAULT
N. INTENT
O. IRRATIONALLY
P. HUB

1. Slipping back
2. Single; only
3. Begging
4. Resolute
5. Attack
6. Customs
7. Having an injured leg or foot
8. Threatening
9. Center
10. One who is under the legal age
11. Twisted out of shape
12. Doubtful; disbelieving
13. Sneering
14. Dealing with people in a skillful way
15. In an uncontrolled, excitable state
16. Not logically

A=	B=	C=	D=
E=	F=	G=	H=
I=	J=	K=	L=
M=	N=	O=	P=

That Was Then, This Is Now Vocabulary Magic Squares 3 Answer Key

Match the definition with the vocabulary word. Put your answers in the magic squares below. When your answers are correct, all columns and rows will add to the same number.

A. SINISTER
B. RELAPSE
C. SMIRKING
D. INCREDULOUS
E. CONTORTED
F. TACTFULLY
G. SOLE
H. LAME
I. MINOR
J. HYSTERICAL
K. PLEADING
L. FORMALITIES
M. ASSAULT
N. INTENT
O. IRRATIONALLY
P. HUB

1. Slipping back
2. Single; only
3. Begging
4. Resolute
5. Attack
6. Customs
7. Having an injured leg or foot
8. Threatening
9. Center
10. One who is under the legal age
11. Twisted out of shape
12. Doubtful; disbelieving
13. Sneering
14. Dealing with people in a skillful way
15. In an uncontrolled, excitable state
16. Not logically

A=8	B=1	C=13	D=12
E=11	F=14	G=2	H=7
I=10	J=15	K=3	L=6
M=5	N=4	O=16	P=9

That Was Then, This Is Now Vocabulary Magic Squares 4

Match the definition with the vocabulary word. Put your answers in the magic squares below. When your answers are correct, all columns and rows will add to the same number.

A. HOSTILITY
B. HYSTERICAL
C. HUB
D. VAGUE
E. PROBATION
F. IRRATIONALLY
G. TAUNTING
H. OBLIGINGLY
I. SASSY
J. FORMALITIES
K. GRAVELY
L. COMMUNE
M. CONTORTED
N. FLOUNCED
O. PLEADING
P. LAME

1. Twisted out of shape
2. Not logically
3. Willingly
4. Begging
5. A group of people living together
6. Center
7. Conflict
8. Customs
9. Seriously
10. Indistinct
11. In an uncontrolled, excitable state
12. Rude
13. Moved in a bouncing or lively in manner
14. Supervised freedom for lawbreakers
15. Insulting; mean teasing
16. Having an injured leg or foot

A=	B=	C=	D=
E=	F=	G=	H=
I=	J=	K=	L=
M=	N=	O=	P=

That Was Then, This Is Now Vocabulary Magic Squares 4 Answer Key

Match the definition with the vocabulary word. Put your answers in the magic squares below. When your answers are correct, all columns and rows will add to the same number.

A. HOSTILITY
B. HYSTERICAL
C. HUB
D. VAGUE
E. PROBATION
F. IRRATIONALLY
G. TAUNTING
H. OBLIGINGLY
I. SASSY
J. FORMALITIES
K. GRAVELY
L. COMMUNE
M. CONTORTED
N. FLOUNCED
O. PLEADING
P. LAME

1. Twisted out of shape
2. Not logically
3. Willingly
4. Begging
5. A group of people living together
6. Center
7. Conflict
8. Customs
9. Seriously
10. Indistinct
11. In an uncontrolled, excitable state
12. Rude
13. Moved in a bouncing or lively in manner
14. Supervised freedom for lawbreakers
15. Insulting; mean teasing
16. Having an injured leg or foot

A=7	B=11	C=6	D=10
E=14	F=2	G=15	H=3
I=12	J=8	K=9	L=5
M=1	N=13	O=4	P=16

That Was Then, This Is Now Vocabulary Word Search 1

Words are placed backwards, forward, diagonally, up and down. Clues listed below can help you find the words. Circle the hidden vocabulary words in the maze.

```
Q K K Y L L A C I T S A C R A S H D N M
P R W Z G M O Y R N F B C H V O E N G R
Z L F S P G B Q F S C D X F S R J N H Z
P Q E L W M L L Z L Y L P T E G F Y A W
F G R A P Y I V J I K S I T F J S R F C
F Z R C D W G P S G R L N N P T L E O J
T M P K R I I I D H I U M R E S A L R B
L A M E D H N O I T A B O R P D N A E P
Q F V D E I G G Y S P F I O R E K P M W
Z S W B S B L N R V O C H N X T Y S E L
Z M M T P S Y J V U A J C I D R T E N D
Y B E I E S G N N L K G H M E O A I T G
Y R X F R P O D M F F Z U M C T U N I C
G M B Y A K F L L V L I I E N N N C O L
D U K N T M I G E T L P N S N U O T R N S
H B L Q E B Q N L Z I T A U O C I E E F
A Q Q F L B G U G S C E S M L O N D D D
B Z R K Y E A R C N K N S M F B G U G Z
R K G L F S Q I C K B T Y O G S B L R D
U M V U S K N R M G K P S C V C K O A F
P H L A B G T A C T F U L Y U F U V Q
T W I T T I C I S M R H R H M R H S E V
L L I R R A T I O N A L L Y T E J X L V
Y F O R M A L I T I E S R L L N W S Y K
G W Y R V B P B W K P K W X T X H J V X
```

A group of people living together (7)
Attack (7)
Begging (8)
Center (3)
Conflict (9)
Customs (11)
Dealing with people in a skillful way (9)
Distance (4)
Doubtful; disbelieving (11)
Having an injured leg or foot (4)
Hopelessly (11)
In a mocking manner (13)
In an uncontrolled, excitable state (10)
Indistinct (5)
Insulting; mean teasing (8)
Intellectual (8)
Joke (9)
Light in form or build (6)
Moved in a bouncing or lively in manner (8)
Not logically (12)

One who is under the legal age (5)
Remembering past events (11)
Resolute (6)
Rude (5)
Said before (14)
Seriously (7)
Single; only (4)
Slipping back (7)
Slowed (7)
Sneering (8)
Strolled (9)
Suddenly (8)
Supervised freedom for lawbreakers (9)
Tall and skinny (5)
Tending (8)
Threatening (8)
Twisted out of shape (9)
Unclear (7)
Wanting to give punishment for a wrong (8)
Willingly (10)

That Was Then, This Is Now Vocabulary Word Search 1 Answer Key

Words are placed backwards, forward, diagonally, up and down. Clues listed below can help you find the words. Circle the hidden vocabulary words in the maze.

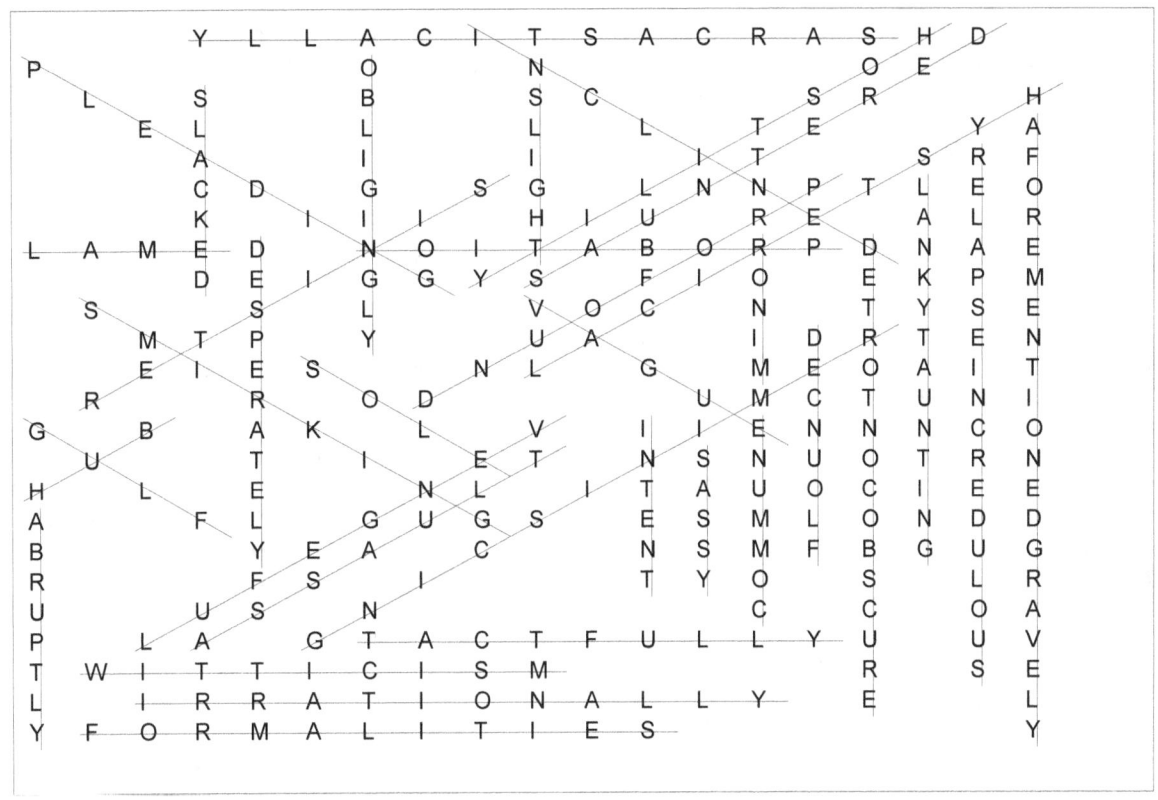

A group of people living together (7)
Attack (7)
Begging (8)
Center (3)
Conflict (9)
Customs (11)
Dealing with people in a skillful way (9)
Distance (4)
Doubtful; disbelieving (11)
Having an injured leg or foot (4)
Hopelessly (11)
In a mocking manner (13)
In an uncontrolled, excitable state (10)
Indistinct (5)
Insulting; mean teasing (8)
Intellectual (8)
Joke (9)
Light in form or build (6)
Moved in a bouncing or lively in manner (8)
Not logically (12)

One who is under the legal age (5)
Remembering past events (11)
Resolute (6)
Rude (5)
Said before (14)
Seriously (7)
Single; only (4)
Slipping back (7)
Slowed (7)
Sneering (8)
Strolled (9)
Suddenly (8)
Supervised freedom for lawbreakers (9)
Tall and skinny (5)
Tending (8)
Threatening (8)
Twisted out of shape (9)
Unclear (7)
Wanting to give punishment for a wrong (8)
Willingly (10)

That Was Then, This Is Now Vocabulary Word Search 2

Words are placed backwards, forward, diagonally, up and down. Clues listed below can help you find the words. Circle the hidden vocabulary words in the maze.

```
S A R C A S T I C A L L Y L O N D W T B
L P G Y M C F Y R G M T S H B G G W T W
M H F L A C I R E T S Y H M L N S N Z G
S O K E K D X F R E T S I N I S H B I B
J S T V Y T Y W B T L W W T G R U V N T
R T W A C V L D G G Q O N M I H K X T M
S I X R C O H E G L B U C I N V S I E N
S L I G H T M K N S A S L N G Y A V N T
K I A J G A F M C T O K B O L V U G T G
C T C C L S C U U N H L Y R Y E N A U Y
C Y R O K Y R G L N J L E E B N T B Q E
P P E H N E D U G L E X P M T G E R S K
P R L Z V T D L G T Y I X I W E R U Y V
L O A S L Y O F A G V R C N C F E P D X
E F P R A X V R S W S R C I S U D T M B
A O S K L S E H T L U A S S A L E L L W
D U E J N P S Z R E N T V C W I C Y A Z
I N W B S Z H Y S O D I H I I N N B N Q
N D L E J T M M I Q D O R N T C U W K J
G H D R T T X T S K N N Y G T L O J Y J
G S H V C T A M Z L S A D R I I L N V Q
W P D G Z B W T P Y L L N B C N F C B X
M W N D O T F O R M A L I T I E S W F G
I N C R E D U L O U S Y W C S D T C N J
N J P S L R D E N O I T N E M E R O F A
```

A group of people living together (7)
Attack (7)
Begging (8)
Center (3)
Conflict (9)
Customs (11)
Dealing with people in a skillful way (9)
Distance (4)
Doubtful; disbelieving (11)
Having an injured leg or foot (4)
Hopelessly (11)
In a mocking manner (13)
In an uncontrolled, excitable state (10)
Indistinct (5)
Insulting; mean teasing (8)
Intellectual (8)
Joke (9)
Light in form or build (6)
Moved in a bouncing or lively in manner (8)
Not logically (12)

One who is under the legal age (5)
Remembering past events (11)
Resolute (6)
Rude (5)
Said before (14)
Seriously (7)
Single; only (4)
Slipping back (7)
Slowed (7)
Sneering (8)
Strolled (9)
Suddenly (8)
Supervised freedom for lawbreakers (9)
Tall and skinny (5)
Tending (8)
Threatening (8)
Twisted out of shape (9)
Unclear (7)
Wanting to give punishment for a wrong (8)
Willingly (10)

That Was Then, This Is Now Vocabulary Word Search 2 Answer Key

Words are placed backwards, forward, diagonally, up and down. Clues listed below can help you find the words. Circle the hidden vocabulary words in the maze.

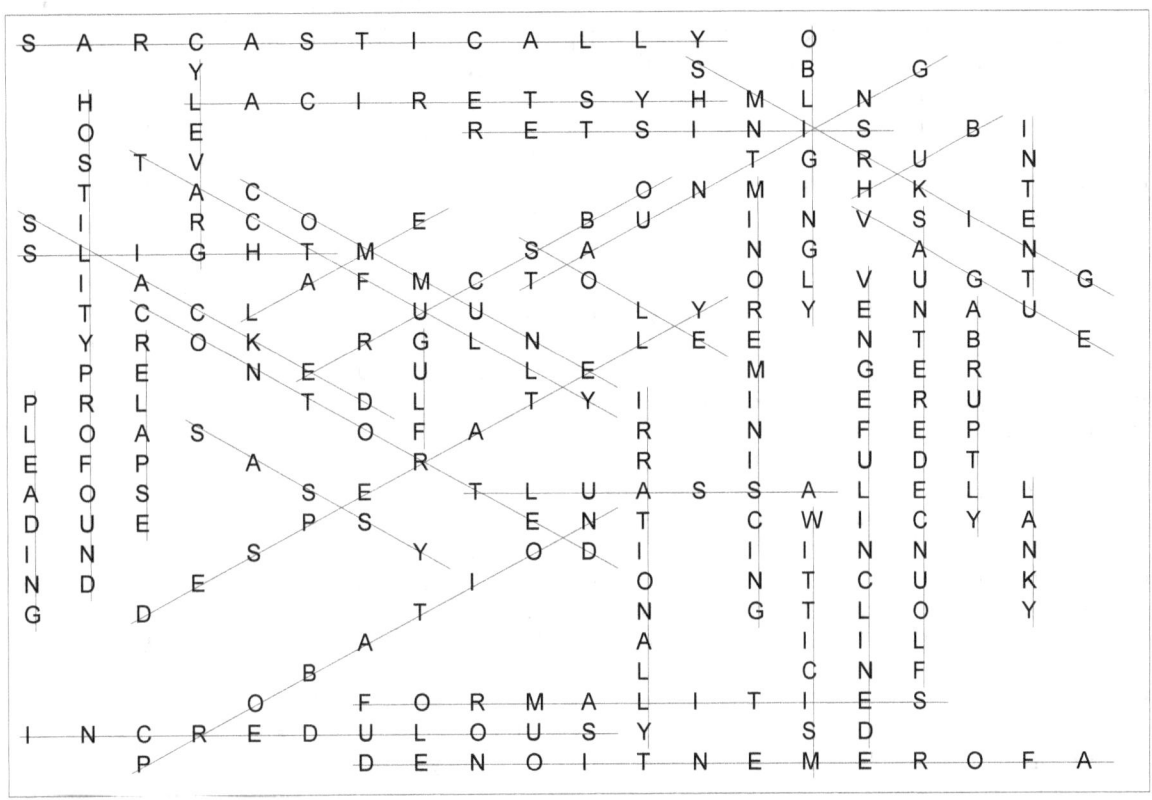

A group of people living together (7)
Attack (7)
Begging (8)
Center (3)
Conflict (9)
Customs (11)
Dealing with people in a skillful way (9)
Distance (4)
Doubtful; disbelieving (11)
Having an injured leg or foot (4)
Hopelessly (11)
In a mocking manner (13)
In an uncontrolled, excitable state (10)
Indistinct (5)
Insulting; mean teasing (8)
Intellectual (8)
Joke (9)
Light in form or build (6)
Moved in a bouncing or lively in manner (8)
Not logically (12)
One who is under the legal age (5)
Remembering past events (11)
Resolute (6)
Rude (5)
Said before (14)
Seriously (7)
Single; only (4)
Slipping back (7)
Slowed (7)
Sneering (8)
Strolled (9)
Suddenly (8)
Supervised freedom for lawbreakers (9)
Tall and skinny (5)
Tending (8)
Threatening (8)
Twisted out of shape (9)
Unclear (7)
Wanting to give punishment for a wrong (8)
Willingly (10)

That Was Then, This Is Now Vocabulary Word Search 3

Words are placed backwards, forward, diagonally, up and down. Words listed below are included in the maze. Circle the hidden vocabulary words in the maze.

```
S C N L W I R R A T I O N A L L Y F G S
M A O B I H Y S T E R I C A L L L O R T
I F I N T I T T P J R N L J L O T A G G
R O T Z T D N V G M X H N A U P P M V S
K R A A I O G C N X Y P C N Y R U A E F
I E B F C H R K R L T I C T M O R L L J
N M O X I T M T E E T E I V T F B I Y W
G E R G S R F T E S D L S J M O A T S Y
G N P J M P A U A D I U P S J U J I N S
X T X N K R N C L T R H L M V N Q E N K
Q I P H E L R F S L G Q C O R D D S I H
K O Q P N A W O T N Y R J D U C F G S Q
P N S W S R H Z I H W M N L D S L T T Q
D E D X N O H C Y H P T S A D P J S E W
D D Z Z K N S T M S A N K M L Q G B R Q
V C Y K S I V A G U E X R E L A P S E N
C C Y F N M R D N S H C A C B A L N Q C
L K Y I Y V N T D D O D S I Y I N M V P
G D M Q I E I Y W Y I L N D G A C K K P
D E R E T N U A S N D C E H M S O L Y M
R L N N G G T Y G K L K T Q A S M L B B
V L D S R E L E Y I C S Z S Y A M T P X
V P Y F H F S S N A L B S H D U U T P Z
N G U L F U J E L T K Y V U H L N Q L B
T W L K J L D S E R U C S B O T E D B V
```

ABRUPTLY
AFOREMENTIONED
ASSAULT
COMMUNE
CONTORTED
DESPERATELY
FLOUNCED
FORMALITIES
GRAVELY
GULF
HOSTILITY
HUB
HYSTERICAL
INCLINED
INCREDULOUS
INTENT
IRRATIONALLY
LAME
LANKY
MINOR
OBSCURE
PLEADING
PROBATION
PROFOUND
RELAPSE
REMINISCING
SARCASTICALLY
SASSY
SAUNTERED
SINISTER
SLACKED
SLIGHT
SMIRKING
SOLE
TACTFULLY
TAUNTING
VAGUE
VENGEFUL
WITTICISM

That Was Then, This Is Now Vocabulary Word Search 3 Answer Key

Words are placed backwards, forward, diagonally, up and down. Words listed below are included in the maze. Circle the hidden vocabulary words in the maze.

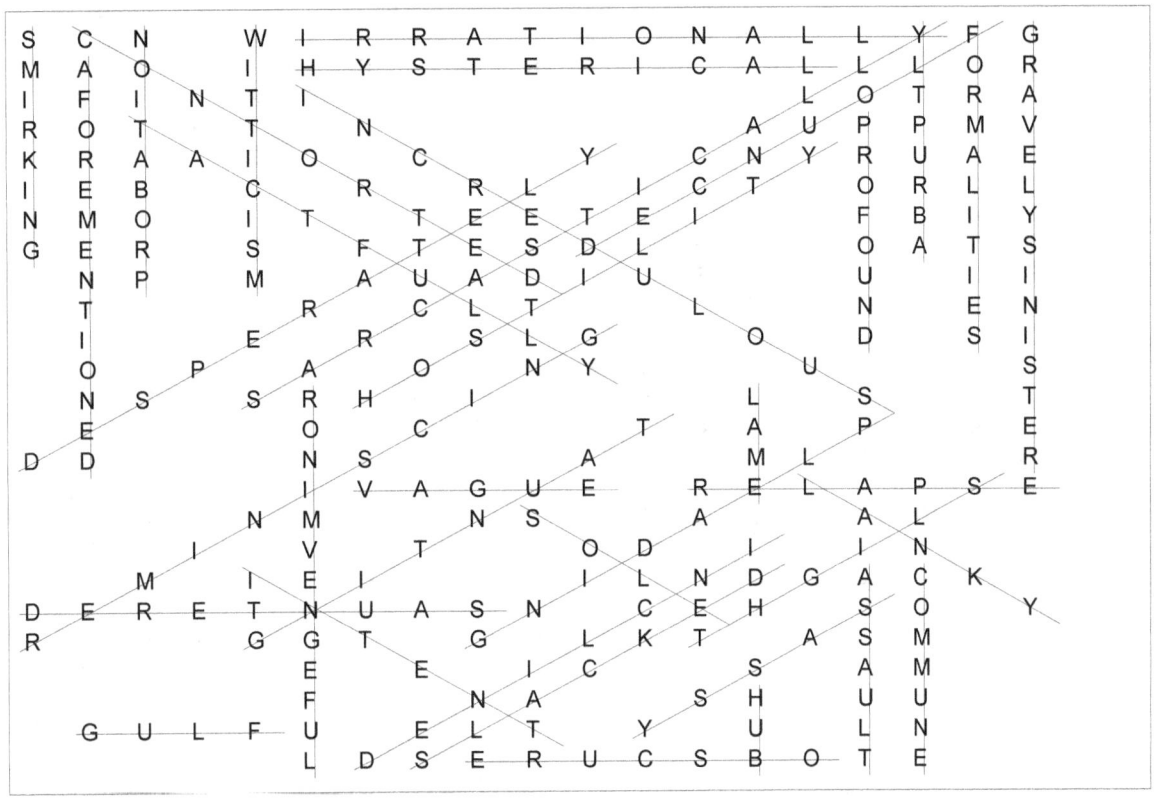

ABRUPTLY	INCLINED	SARCASTICALLY
AFOREMENTIONED	INCREDULOUS	SASSY
ASSAULT	INTENT	SAUNTERED
COMMUNE	IRRATIONALLY	SINISTER
CONTORTED	LAME	SLACKED
DESPERATELY	LANKY	SLIGHT
FLOUNCED	MINOR	SMIRKING
FORMALITIES	OBSCURE	SOLE
GRAVELY	PLEADING	TACTFULLY
GULF	PROBATION	TAUNTING
HOSTILITY	PROFOUND	VAGUE
HUB	RELAPSE	VENGEFUL
HYSTERICAL	REMINISCING	WITTICISM

That Was Then, This Is Now Vocabulary Word Search 4

Words are placed backwards, forward, diagonally, up and down. Words listed below are included in the maze. Circle the hidden vocabulary words in the maze.

```
P R O B A T I O N O B L I G I N G L Y N
O L Q U T L N C N R A N I F R S P N X J
C B E H X N C N X N E H R D G A P L J V
V O S A A Y F Q K K G R L D T V R C Y Y
A S M C D B V Y Y L E T A R E P S E D N
G A L M U I R X Z V J C T P L H A M L N
U S F A U R N U T T I K T R S S R I U Y
E S G R C N E G P R M D O M I E C N F W
I A F Z N K E X E T E L N Z N I A I E V
N U B K J N E T B T L V A B C T S S G Y
C L Y S N V S D R V T Y L K L I T C N J
R T C H T Y X O T D A Q L Q I L I I E P
E R Q L H B T J E C Z Y W N A C N V Y
D E R E T N U A S N T J T V E M A G G N
U G W T O K V F Z O F J D S D R L F F L
L T I C Z T Y G Y I U P G M C O L P L L
O F T G X Y L T V T L D T I J F Y J O M
U N T R W M I W L N L F A R K R H K U D
S V I Z P L I L Y E Y C U K G R S Q N Y
S H C W I F N N L M J G N I M G O T C Y
Q A I T J C X H O E R U T N N Y L N E Y
W K S I N I S T E R S L I G H T E V D H
B O M S H H Q R B O V F N F R M E H F P
H W H S Y H N W N F B W G R A G K N Q W
P R O F O U N D H A D B V L Y J T Y T X
```

ABRUPTLY
AFOREMENTIONED
ASSAULT
COMMUNE
CONTORTED
DESPERATELY
FLOUNCED
FORMALITIES
GRAVELY
GULF
HOSTILITY
HUB
HYSTERICAL
INCLINED

INCREDULOUS
INTENT
IRRATIONALLY
LAME
LANKY
MINOR
OBLIGINGLY
OBSCURE
PLEADING
PROBATION
PROFOUND
RELAPSE
REMINISCING
SARCASTICALLY

SASSY
SAUNTERED
SINISTER
SLACKED
SLIGHT
SMIRKING
SOLE
TACTFULLY
TAUNTING
VAGUE
VENGEFUL
WITTICISM

That Was Then, This Is Now Vocabulary Word Search 4 Answer Key

Words are placed backwards, forward, diagonally, up and down. Words listed below are included in the maze. Circle the hidden vocabulary words in the maze.

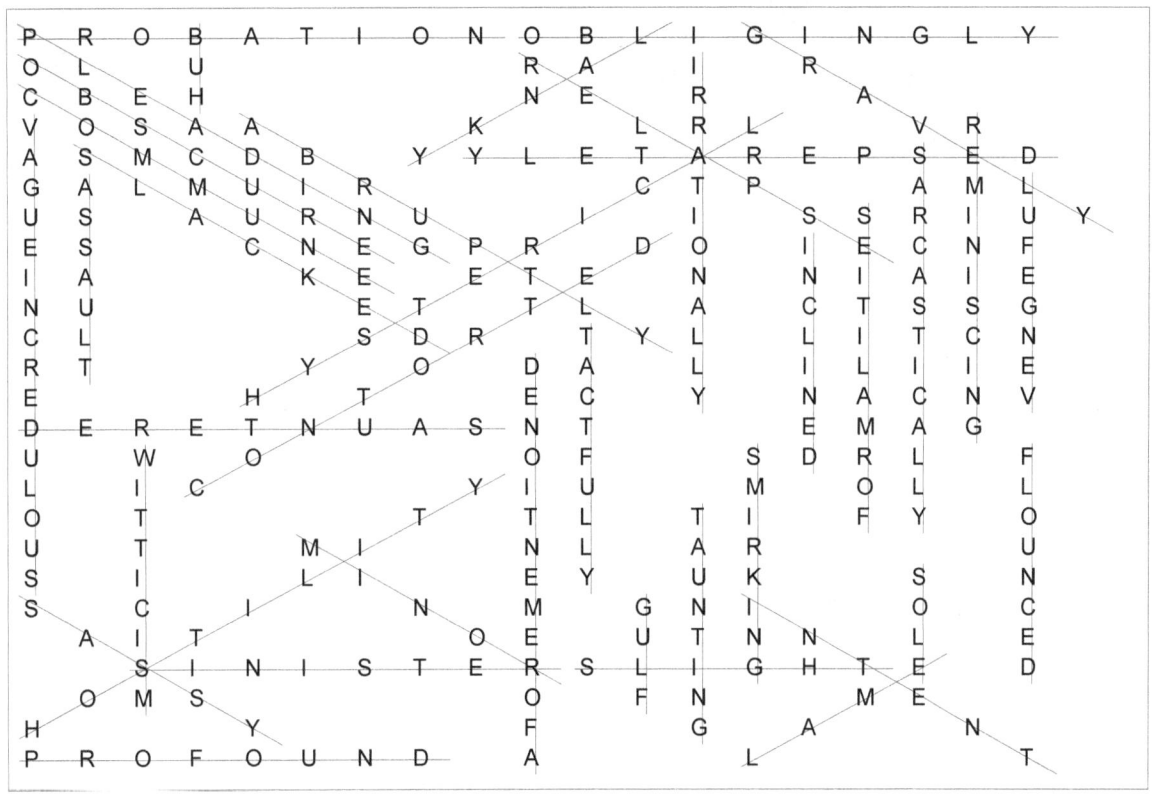

ABRUPTLY	INCREDULOUS	SASSY
AFOREMENTIONED	INTENT	SAUNTERED
ASSAULT	IRRATIONALLY	SINISTER
COMMUNE	LAME	SLACKED
CONTORTED	LANKY	SLIGHT
DESPERATELY	MINOR	SMIRKING
FLOUNCED	OBLIGINGLY	SOLE
FORMALITIES	OBSCURE	TACTFULLY
GRAVELY	PLEADING	TAUNTING
GULF	PROBATION	VAGUE
HOSTILITY	PROFOUND	VENGEFUL
HUB	RELAPSE	WITTICISM
HYSTERICAL	REMINISCING	
INCLINED	SARCASTICALLY	

That Was Then, This Is Now Vocabulary Crossword 1

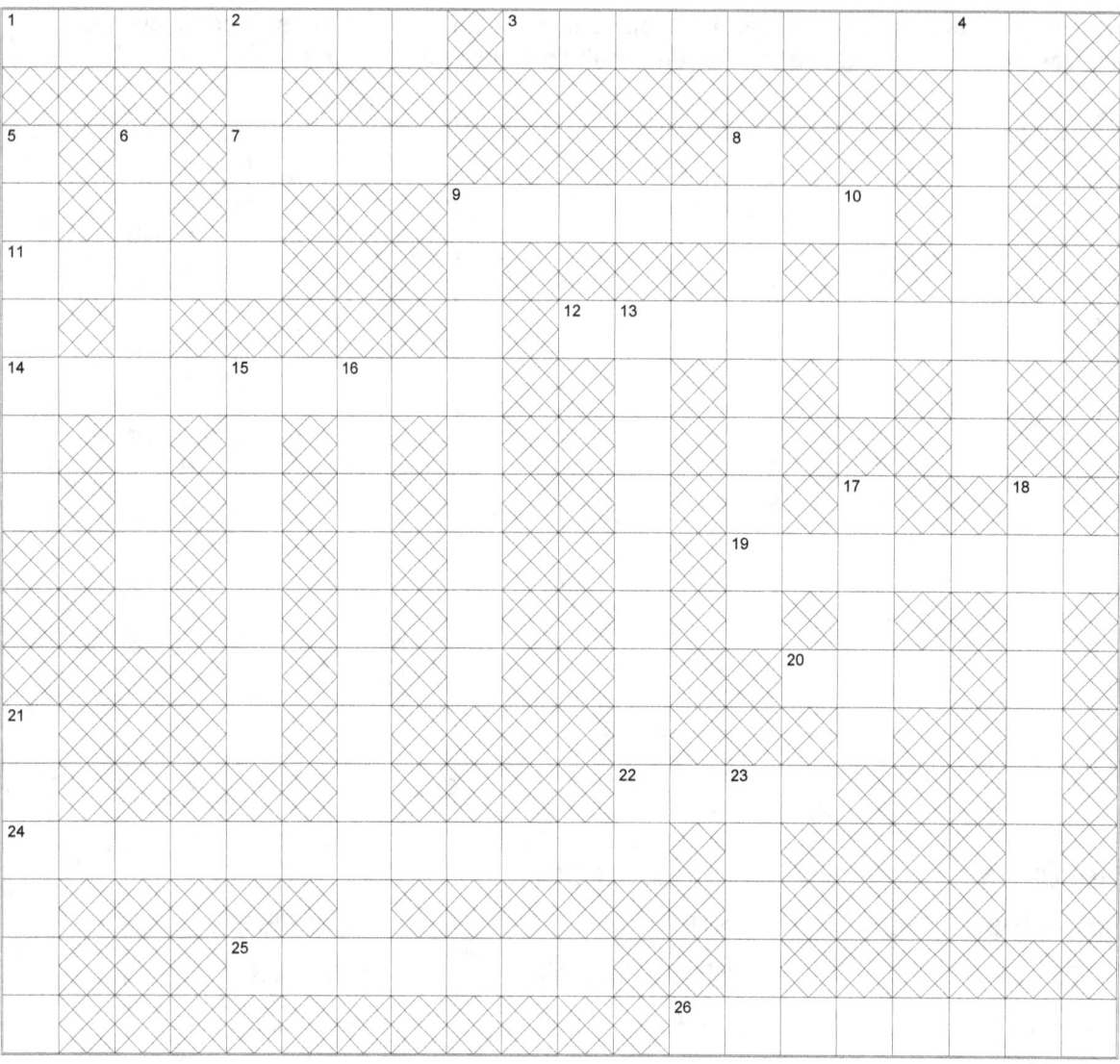

Across
1. Threatening
3. In an uncontrolled, excitable state
7. Single; only
9. Sneering
11. Tall and skinny
12. Conflict
14. Supervised freedom for lawbreakers
19. Slowed
20. Center
22. Having an injured leg or foot
24. Not logically
25. Unclear
26. Intellectual

Down
2. Rude
4. Suddenly
5. Slipping back
6. Twisted out of shape
8. Joke
9. Strolled
10. Distance
13. Willingly
15. Attack
16. Doubtful; disbelieving
17. Indistinct
18. Wanting to give punishment for a wrong
21. Light in form or build
23. One who is under the legal age

That Was Then, This Is Now Vocabulary Crossword 1 Answer Key

	1 S	I	N	I	2 S	T	E	R		3 H	Y	S	T	E	R	I	C	4 A	L	
					A													B		
	5 R		6 C		7 S	O	L	E					8 W					R		
	E		O		S				9 S	M	I	R	K	I	N	10 G		U		
	11 L	A	N	K	Y				A				T			U		P		
	A		T					12 U	13 H	O	S	T	I	L	I	T	Y		
	14 P	R	O	B	15 A	T	16 I	O	N			B		I		F		L		
	S		R		S		N		T			L		C			17		18	
	E		T		S		C		E			I		I			V		V	
			E		A		R		R			G		19 S	L	A	C	K	E	D
			D		U		E		E			I		M			G		N	
					L		D		D			N		20 H	U	B			G	
	21 S				T		U					G			E				E	
	L						L					22 L	A	23 M	E				F	
	24 I	R	R	A	T	I	O	N	A	L	L	Y		I					U	
	G						U							N					L	
	H				25 O	B	S	C	U	R	E			O						
	T										26 P	R	O	F	O	U	N	D		

Across
1. Threatening
3. In an uncontrolled, excitable state
7. Single; only
9. Sneering
11. Tall and skinny
12. Conflict
14. Supervised freedom for lawbreakers
19. Slowed
20. Center
22. Having an injured leg or foot
24. Not logically
25. Unclear
26. Intellectual

Down
2. Rude
4. Suddenly
5. Slipping back
6. Twisted out of shape
8. Joke
9. Strolled
10. Distance
13. Willingly
15. Attack
16. Doubtful; disbelieving
17. Indistinct
18. Wanting to give punishment for a wrong
21. Light in form or build
23. One who is under the legal age

That Was Then, This Is Now Vocabulary Crossword 2

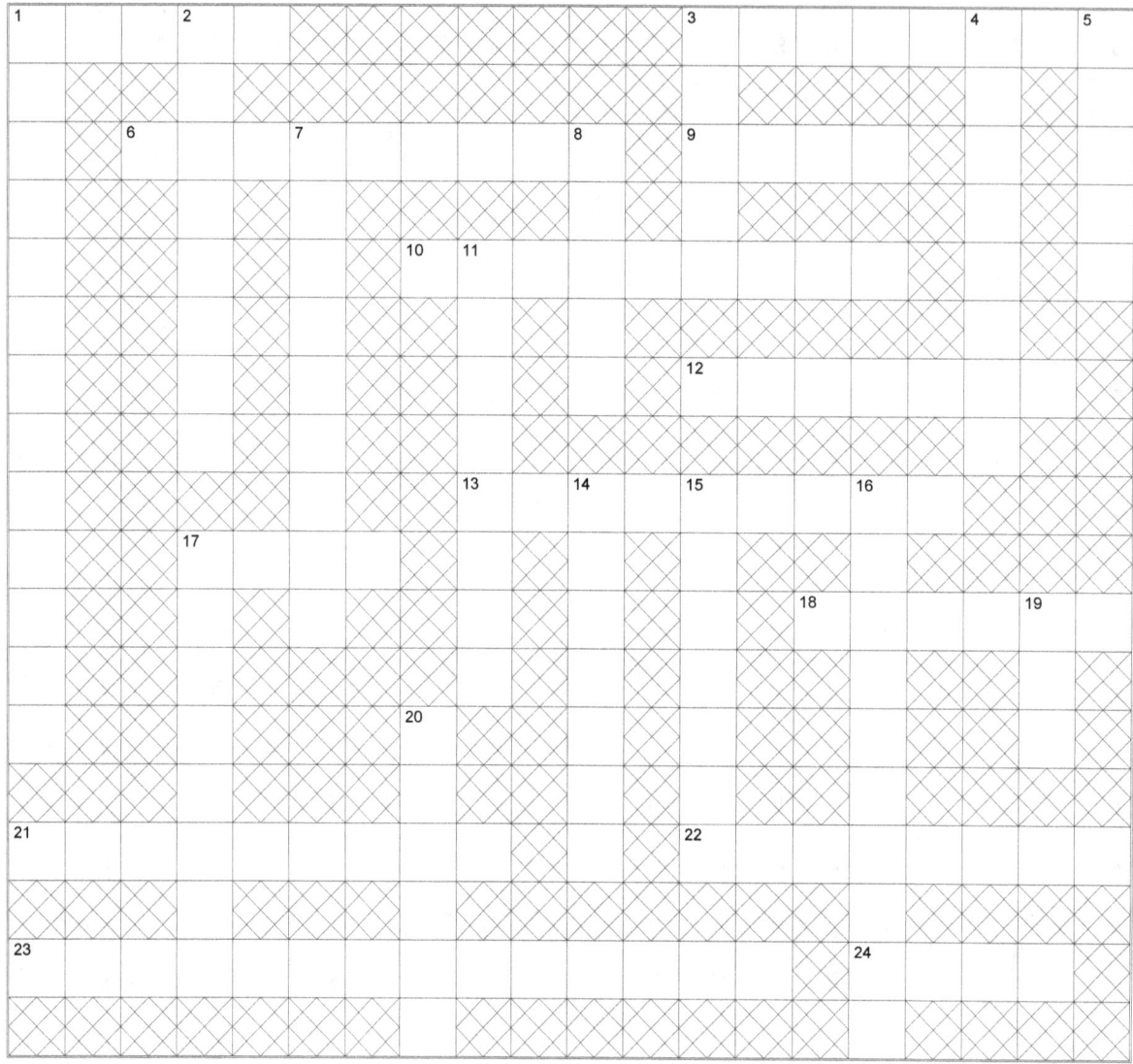

Across
1. Rude
3. Wanting to give punishment for a wrong
6. Joke
9. Distance
10. Strolled
12. Slowed
13. Supervised freedom for lawbreakers
17. Single; only
18. Light in form or build
21. Conflict
22. Insulting; mean teasing
23. Said before
24. Having an injured leg or foot

Down
1. In a mocking manner
2. Sneering
3. Indistinct
4. Moved in a bouncing or lively in manner
5. Tall and skinny
7. Dealing with people in a skillful way
8. One who is under the legal age
11. Suddenly
14. Unclear
15. Attack
16. Willingly
17. Threatening
19. Center
20. Resolute

That Was Then, This Is Now Vocabulary Crossword 2 Answer Key

	1 S	A	2 S	Y					3 V	E	N	G	E	4 F	U	5 L
	A		M						A					L		A
	R		6 W	I	7 T	I	C	I	8 S	M	9 G	U	L	F		O	N
	C			R		A				I		U				U	K
	A			K		C		10 S	11 A	U	N	T	E	R	E	D		N	Y
	S			I		T			B			O					C	
	T			N		F			R			R		12 S	L	A	C	K	E	D
	I			G		U			U								D	
	C					L			13 P	R	14 O	B	15 A	T	16 I	O	N
	A		17 S	O	L	E		T		B		S		B		
	L		I		Y		L		S		S	18 S	L	19 I	G	H	T
	L		N				Y		C		A		I		U	
	Y		I			20 I		U		U		G		B	
			S			N		R		L		I			
21 H	O	S	T	I	L	I	T	Y		22 T	A	U	N	T	I	N	G
			E			E				C				
23 A	F	O	R	E	M	E	N	T	I	O	N	E	D	24 L	A	M	E
						T							Y			

Across
1. Rude
3. Wanting to give punishment for a wrong
6. Joke
9. Distance
10. Strolled
12. Slowed
13. Supervised freedom for lawbreakers
17. Single; only
18. Light in form or build
21. Conflict
22. Insulting; mean teasing
23. Said before
24. Having an injured leg or foot

Down
1. In a mocking manner
2. Sneering
3. Indistinct
4. Moved in a bouncing or lively in manner
5. Tall and skinny
7. Dealing with people in a skillful way
8. One who is under the legal age
11. Suddenly
14. Unclear
15. Attack
16. Willingly
17. Threatening
19. Center
20. Resolute

That Was Then, This Is Now Vocabulary Crossword 3

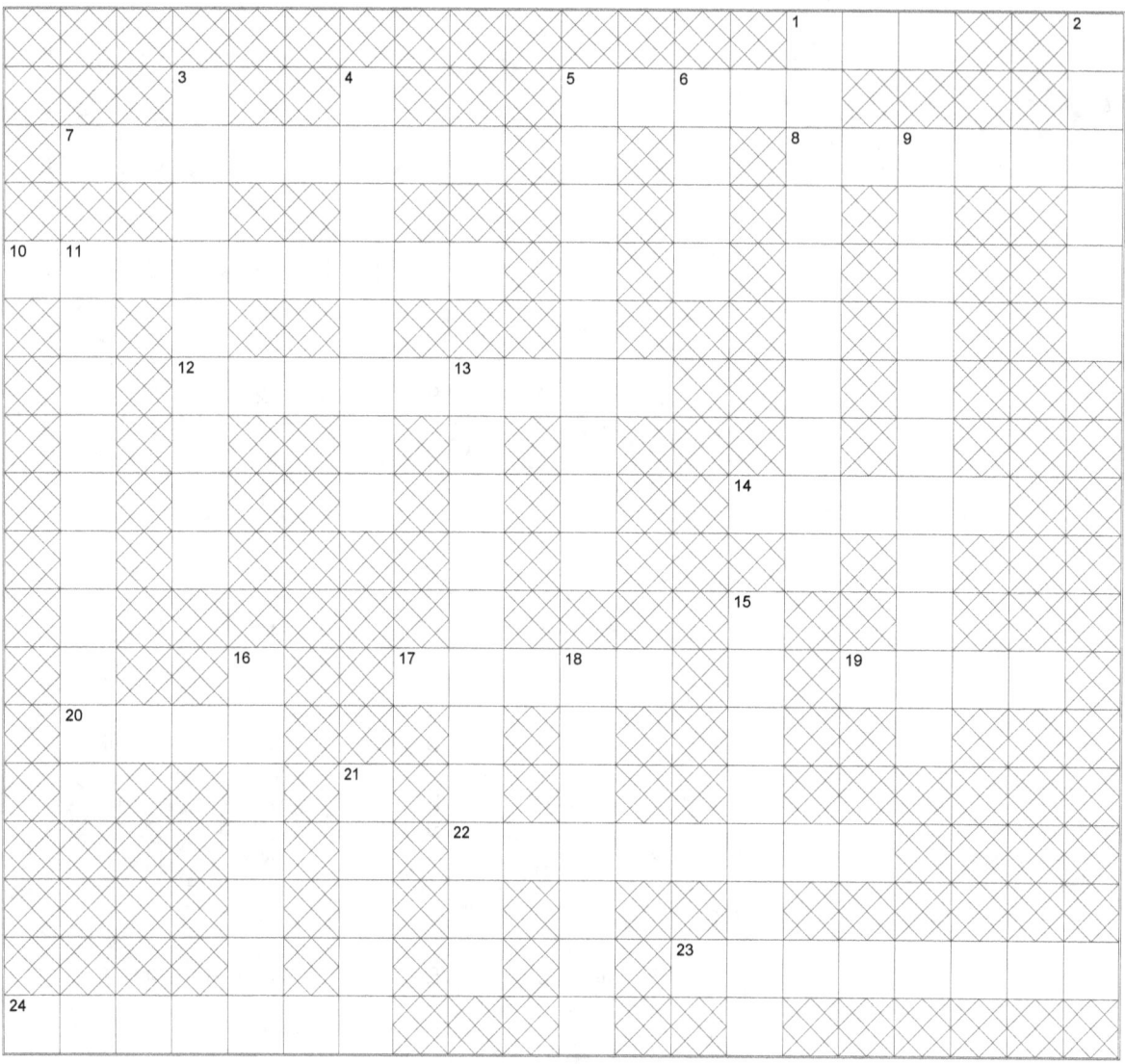

Across
1. Center
5. Rude
7. Sneering
8. Light in form or build
10. Conflict
12. Twisted out of shape
14. Indistinct
17. One who is under the legal age
19. Distance
20. Having an injured leg or foot
22. Tending
23. Wanting to give punishment for a wrong
24. Seriously

Down
1. In an uncontrolled, excitable state
2. Resolute
3. Joke
4. Threatening
5. Strolled
6. Single; only
9. Doubtful; disbelieving
11. Willingly
13. Remembering past events
15. Moved in a bouncing or lively in manner
16. Slipping back
18. Unclear
21. Tall and skinny

That Was Then, This Is Now Vocabulary Crossword 3 Answer Key

								1 H	U	B		2 I
		3 W		4 S		5 S	6 A	S	S	Y		N
	7 S	M	I	R	K	I	N	G		8 S	9 L	I	G	H	T
		T		N		A		O		T	N		E
10 H	11 O	S	T	I	L	I	T	Y		E	L	E	C		N
	B	I		S		T		E		R	R		T
	L	12 C	O	N	T	13 O	R	T	E	D		I	E	
	I	I		E		R		E		C	D	
	G	S		R		M		E		14 V	A	G	U	E
	I	M				I		D		L		L
	N					N				15 F		O
	G	16 R		17 M	I	18 N	O	R		19 G	U	L	F
20 L	A	M	E			S		B		O		S
	Y		L	21 L		C		S		U
		A		A	22 I	N	C	L	I	N	E	D
		P		N		N		U		C
		S		K		G		R		23 V	E	N	G	E	F	U	L
24 G	R	A	V	E	L	Y				E		D

Across
1. Center
5. Rude
7. Sneering
8. Light in form or build
10. Conflict
12. Twisted out of shape
14. Indistinct
17. One who is under the legal age
19. Distance
20. Having an injured leg or foot
22. Tending
23. Wanting to give punishment for a wrong
24. Seriously

Down
1. In an uncontrolled, excitable state
2. Resolute
3. Joke
4. Threatening
5. Strolled
6. Single; only
9. Doubtful; disbelieving
11. Willingly
13. Remembering past events
15. Moved in a bouncing or lively in manner
16. Slipping back
18. Unclear
21. Tall and skinny

That Was Then, This Is Now Vocabulary Crossword 4

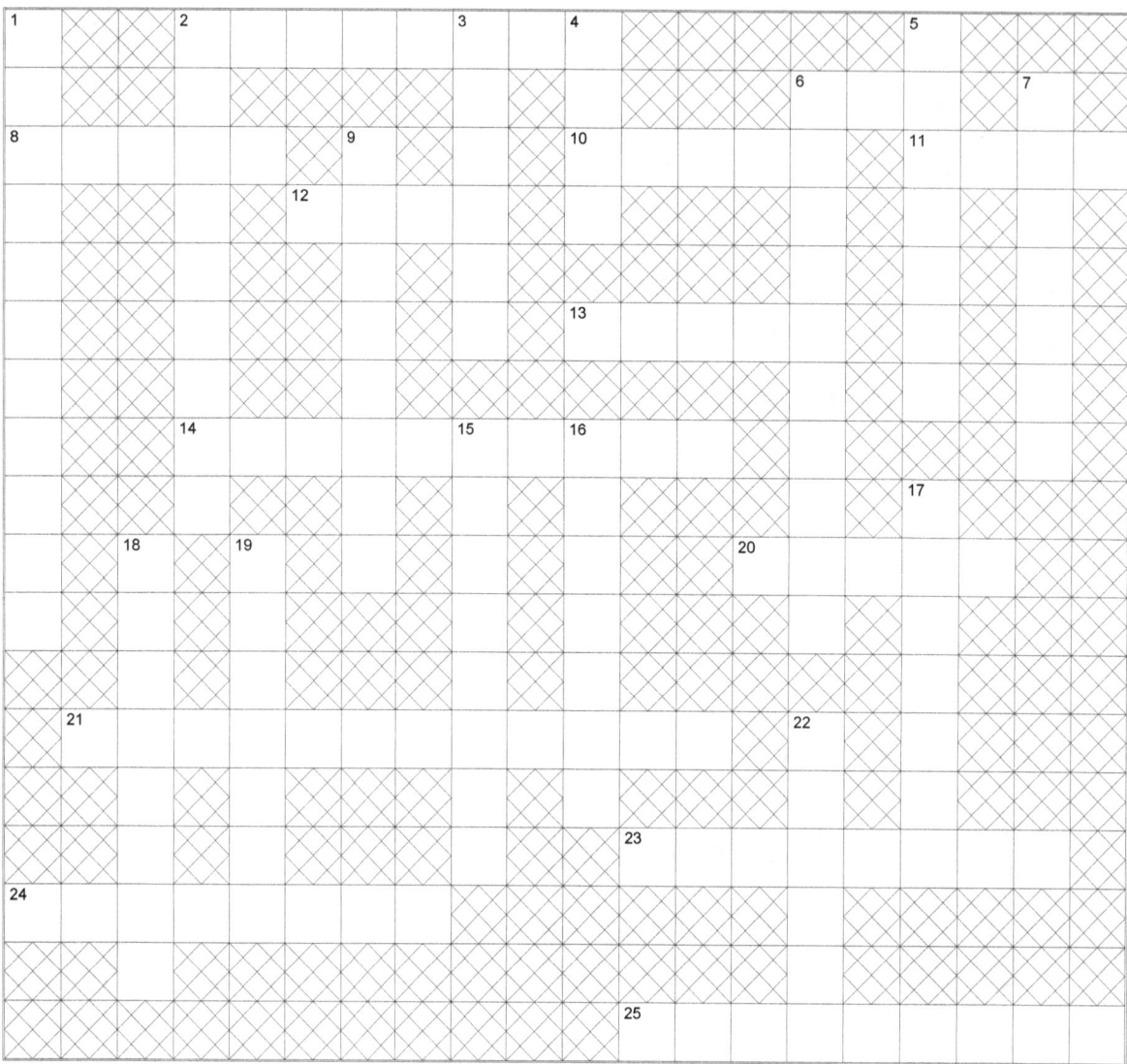

Across
2. Begging
6. Center
8. One who is under the legal age
10. Tall and skinny
11. Single; only
12. Having an injured leg or foot
13. Indistinct
14. Willingly
20. Rude
21. Not logically
23. Threatening
24. Wanting to give punishment for a wrong
25. Dealing with people in a skillful way

Down
1. Remembering past events
2. Supervised freedom for lawbreakers
3. Resolute
4. Distance
5. Unclear
6. In an uncontrolled, excitable state
7. Slowed
9. Insulting; mean teasing
15. Tending
16. Seriously
17. Attack
18. Sneering
19. Slipping back
22. Light in form or build

That Was Then, This Is Now Vocabulary Crossword 4 Answer Key

Across
- 2. Begging
- 6. Center
- 8. One who is under the legal age
- 10. Tall and skinny
- 11. Single; only
- 12. Having an injured leg or foot
- 13. Indistinct
- 14. Willingly
- 20. Rude
- 21. Not logically
- 23. Threatening
- 24. Wanting to give punishment for a wrong
- 25. Dealing with people in a skillful way

Down
- 1. Remembering past events
- 2. Supervised freedom for lawbreakers
- 3. Resolute
- 4. Distance
- 5. Unclear
- 6. In an uncontrolled, excitable state
- 7. Slowed
- 9. Insulting; mean teasing
- 15. Tending
- 16. Seriously
- 17. Attack
- 18. Sneering
- 19. Slipping back
- 22. Light in form or build

That Was Then, This Is Now Vocabulary Juggle Letters 1

1. CTLAFYTLU = 1. _____
   Dealing with people in a skillful way

2. ATLOREIMFIS = 2. _____
   Customs

3. GITSHL = 3. _____
   Light in form or build

4. OFDLUCNE = 4. _____
   Moved in a bouncing or lively in manner

5. ASYSS = 5. _____
   Rude

6. LVUFNEGE = 6. _____
   Wanting to give punishment for a wrong

7. SIIRNIEGMNC = 7. _____
   Remembering past events

8. CUEDLRNIUOS = 8. _____
   Doubtful; disbelieving

9. MIRKSGIN = 9. _____
   Sneering

10. IDELPANG =10. _____
    Begging

11. ETIISNSR =11. _____
    Threatening

12. ECINNDIL =12. _____
    Tending

13. URTYLBAP =13. _____
    Suddenly

14. MEAL =14. _____
    Having an injured leg or foot

15. LLONYTIARIRA =15. _____
    Not logically

That Was Then, This Is Now Vocabulary Juggle Letters 1 Answer Key

1. CTLAFYTLU = 1. TACTFULLY
   Dealing with people in a skillful way

2. ATLOREIMFIS = 2. FORMALITIES
   Customs

3. GITSHL = 3. SLIGHT
   Light in form or build

4. OFDLUCNE = 4. FLOUNCED
   Moved in a bouncing or lively in manner

5. ASYSS = 5. SASSY
   Rude

6. LVUFNEGE = 6. VENGEFUL
   Wanting to give punishment for a wrong

7. SIIRNIEGMNC = 7. REMINISCING
   Remembering past events

8. CUEDLRNIUOS = 8. INCREDULOUS
   Doubtful; disbelieving

9. MIRKSGIN = 9. SMIRKING
   Sneering

10. IDELPANG = 10. PLEADING
    Begging

11. ETIISNSR = 11. SINISTER
    Threatening

12. ECINNDIL = 12. INCLINED
    Tending

13. URTYLBAP = 13. ABRUPTLY
    Suddenly

14. MEAL = 14. LAME
    Having an injured leg or foot

15. LLONYTIARIRA = 15. IRRATIONALLY
    Not logically

That Was Then, This Is Now Vocabulary Juggle Letters 2

1. KDLSAEC = 1. _____
Slowed

2. ULGF = 2. _____
Distance

3. LRSTHICEYA = 3. _____
In an uncontrolled, excitable state

4. UOENMMC = 4. _____
A group of people living together

5. CTLULTYAF = 5. _____
Dealing with people in a skillful way

6. OTNRAPBIO = 6. _____
Supervised freedom for lawbreakers

7. IIGRMNSK = 7. _____
Sneering

8. TEINTN = 8. _____
Resolute

9. NIINECLD = 9. _____
Tending

10. SSYSA =10. _____
Rude

11. TEUADESRN =11. _____
Strolled

12. OESL =12. _____
Single; only

13. VGRALYE =13. _____
Seriously

14. TGANTIUN =14. _____
Insulting; mean teasing

15. HSTGLI =15. _____
Light in form or build

That Was Then, This Is Now Vocabulary Juggle Letters 2 Answer Key

1. KDLSAEC = 1. SLACKED
Slowed

2. ULGF = 2. GULF
Distance

3. LRSTHICEYA = 3. HYSTERICAL
In an uncontrolled, excitable state

4. UOENMMC = 4. COMMUNE
A group of people living together

5. CTLULTYAF = 5. TACTFULLY
Dealing with people in a skillful way

6. OTNRAPBIO = 6. PROBATION
Supervised freedom for lawbreakers

7. IIGRMNSK = 7. SMIRKING
Sneering

8. TEINTN = 8. INTENT
Resolute

9. NIINECLD = 9. INCLINED
Tending

10. SSYSA = 10. SASSY
Rude

11. TEUADESRN = 11. SAUNTERED
Strolled

12. OESL = 12. SOLE
Single; only

13. VGRALYE = 13. GRAVELY
Seriously

14. TGANTIUN = 14. TAUNTING
Insulting; mean teasing

15. HSTGLI = 15. SLIGHT
Light in form or build

That Was Then, This Is Now Vocabulary Juggle Letters 3

1. RUPFONDO = 1. _____
   Intellectual

2. LENGDPAI = 2. _____
   Begging

3. NNGMCIEISRI = 3. _____
   Remembering past events

4. CLEDKAS = 4. _____
   Slowed

5. LSOE = 5. _____
   Single; only

6. LFGU = 6. _____
   Distance

7. LAEM = 7. _____
   Having an injured leg or foot

8. INTNUGTA = 8. _____
   Insulting; mean teasing

9. MIKGNISR = 9. _____
   Sneering

10. RNOMOAETEDEINF =10. _____
    Said before

11. IENNLDCI =11. _____
    Tending

12. EENDRSUAT =12. _____
    Strolled

13. LNGUEEFV =13. _____
    Wanting to give punishment for a wrong

14. VUGEA =14. _____
    Indistinct

15. ORIBAONTP =15. _____
    Supervised freedom for lawbreakers

That Was Then, This Is Now Vocabulary Juggle Letters 3 Answer Key

1. RUPFONDO = 1. PROFOUND
Intellectual

2. LENGDPAI = 2. PLEADING
Begging

3. NNGMCIEISRI = 3. REMINISCING
Remembering past events

4. CLEDKAS = 4. SLACKED
Slowed

5. LSOE = 5. SOLE
Single; only

6. LFGU = 6. GULF
Distance

7. LAEM = 7. LAME
Having an injured leg or foot

8. INTNUGTA = 8. TAUNTING
Insulting; mean teasing

9. MIKGNISR = 9. SMIRKING
Sneering

10. RNOMOAETEDEINF = 10. AFOREMENTIONED
Said before

11. IENNLDCI = 11. INCLINED
Tending

12. EENDRSUAT = 12. SAUNTERED
Strolled

13. LNGUEEFV = 13. VENGEFUL
Wanting to give punishment for a wrong

14. VUGEA = 14. VAGUE
Indistinct

15. ORIBAONTP = 15. PROBATION
Supervised freedom for lawbreakers

That Was Then, This Is Now Vocabulary Juggle Letters 4

1. GLUVNEFE = 1. _____
   Wanting to give punishment for a wrong

2. INROM = 2. _____
   One who is under the legal age

3. ALIRASSCCAYLT = 3. _____
   In a mocking manner

4. TASEERDYPEL = 4. _____
   Hopelessly

5. VYERLAG = 5. _____
   Seriously

6. KIIMNSGR = 6. _____
   Sneering

7. UTCYLTLFA = 7. _____
   Dealing with people in a skillful way

8. AEUVG = 8. _____
   Indistinct

9. ETINNT = 9. _____
   Resolute

10. YARBTPLU =10. _____
    Suddenly

11. BUH =11. _____
    Center

12. YIIOTTHLS =12. _____
    Conflict

13. DRCNIOSLUUE =13. _____
    Doubtful; disbelieving

14. LGNEPADI =14. _____
    Begging

15. UREOCBS =15. _____
    Unclear

That Was Then, This Is Now Vocabulary Juggle Letters 4 Answer Key

1. GLUVNEFE = 1. VENGEFUL
   Wanting to give punishment for a wrong

2. INROM = 2. MINOR
   One who is under the legal age

3. ALIRASSCCAYLT = 3. SARCASTICALLY
   In a mocking manner

4. TASEERDYPEL = 4. DESPERATELY
   Hopelessly

5. VYERLAG = 5. GRAVELY
   Seriously

6. KIIMNSGR = 6. SMIRKING
   Sneering

7. UTCYLTLFA = 7. TACTFULLY
   Dealing with people in a skillful way

8. AEUVG = 8. VAGUE
   Indistinct

9. ETINNT = 9. INTENT
   Resolute

10. YARBTPLU = 10. ABRUPTLY
    Suddenly

11. BUH = 11. HUB
    Center

12. YIIOTTHLS = 12. HOSTILITY
    Conflict

13. DRCNIOSLUUE = 13. INCREDULOUS
    Doubtful; disbelieving

14. LGNEPADI = 14. PLEADING
    Begging

15. UREOCBS = 15. OBSCURE
    Unclear

ABRUPTLY	Suddenly
AFOREMENTIONED	Said before
ASSAULT	Attack
COMMUNE	A group of people living together
CONTORTED	Twisted out of shape
DESPERATELY	Hopelessly

FLOUNCED	Moved in a bouncing or lively in manner
FORMALITIES	Customs
GRAVELY	Seriously
GULF	Distance
HOSTILITY	Conflict
HUB	Center

HYSTERICAL	In an uncontrolled, excitable state
INCLINED	Tending
INCREDULOUS	Doubtful; disbelieving
INTENT	Resolute
IRRATIONALLY	Not logically
LAME	Having an injured leg or foot

LANKY	Tall and skinny
MINOR	One who is under the legal age
OBLIGINGLY	Willingly
OBSCURE	Unclear
PLEADING	Begging
PROBATION	Supervised freedom for lawbreakers

PROFOUND	Intellectual
RELAPSE	Slipping back
REMINISCING	Remembering past events
SARCASTICALLY	In a mocking manner
SASSY	Rude
SAUNTERED	Strolled

SINISTER	Threatening
SLACKED	Slowed
SLIGHT	Light in form or build
SMIRKING	Sneering
SOLE	Single; only
TACTFULLY	Dealing with people in a skillful way

TAUNTING	Insulting; mean teasing
VAGUE	Indistinct
VENGEFUL	Wanting to give punishment for a wrong
WITTICISM	Joke

That Was Then, This Is Now Vocabulary

OBLIGINGLY	IRRATIONALLY	GULF	PROFOUND	RELAPSE
FLOUNCED	ABRUPTLY	REMINISCING	PROBATION	TACTFULLY
SOLE	HUB	FREE SPACE	SLACKED	COMMUNE
ASSAULT	AFOREMENTIONED	LANKY	OBSCURE	SAUNTERED
SINISTER	FORMALITIES	GRAVELY	HOSTILITY	VAGUE

That Was Then, This Is Now Vocabulary

TAUNTING	LAME	SLIGHT	CONTORTED	INCLINED
PLEADING	SMIRKING	INCREDULOUS	INTENT	DESPERATELY
WITTICISM	SARCASTICALLY	FREE SPACE	VENGEFUL	HYSTERICAL
VAGUE	HOSTILITY	GRAVELY	FORMALITIES	SINISTER
SAUNTERED	OBSCURE	LANKY	AFOREMENTIONED	ASSAULT

That Was Then, This Is Now Vocabulary

TACTFULLY	INCREDULOUS	PROFOUND	PLEADING	AFOREMENTIONED
FLOUNCED	VENGEFUL	ASSAULT	SARCASTICALLY	WITTICISM
SAUNTERED	IRRATIONALLY	FREE SPACE	HOSTILITY	SMIRKING
INTENT	REMINISCING	INCLINED	LAME	SLACKED
FORMALITIES	RELAPSE	DESPERATELY	COMMUNE	SOLE

That Was Then, This Is Now Vocabulary

TAUNTING	HUB	GRAVELY	PROBATION	ABRUPTLY
CONTORTED	MINOR	OBSCURE	SINISTER	HYSTERICAL
SLIGHT	VAGUE	FREE SPACE	LANKY	OBLIGINGLY
SOLE	COMMUNE	DESPERATELY	RELAPSE	FORMALITIES
SLACKED	LAME	INCLINED	REMINISCING	INTENT

That Was Then, This Is Now Vocabulary

SMIRKING	RELAPSE	SARCASTICALLY	INCREDULOUS	SLACKED
COMMUNE	SOLE	INTENT	DESPERATELY	MINOR
LAME	TACTFULLY	FREE SPACE	SLIGHT	ABRUPTLY
VENGEFUL	INCLINED	VAGUE	PROFOUND	LANKY
FORMALITIES	PROBATION	SINISTER	IRRATIONALLY	SASSY

That Was Then, This Is Now Vocabulary

AFOREMENTIONED	SAUNTERED	ASSAULT	TAUNTING	REMINISCING
FLOUNCED	HOSTILITY	OBSCURE	OBLIGINGLY	WITTICISM
CONTORTED	GULF	FREE SPACE	HYSTERICAL	PLEADING
SASSY	IRRATIONALLY	SINISTER	PROBATION	FORMALITIES
LANKY	PROFOUND	VAGUE	INCLINED	VENGEFUL

That Was Then, This Is Now Vocabulary

SINISTER	HYSTERICAL	SLACKED	SASSY	INCLINED
VENGEFUL	AFOREMENTIONED	INCREDULOUS	SAUNTERED	REMINISCING
HUB	GRAVELY	FREE SPACE	SMIRKING	OBLIGINGLY
TACTFULLY	WITTICISM	SARCASTICALLY	CONTORTED	HOSTILITY
FORMALITIES	SOLE	COMMUNE	INTENT	VAGUE

That Was Then, This Is Now Vocabulary

TAUNTING	OBSCURE	ASSAULT	IRRATIONALLY	ABRUPTLY
LAME	RELAPSE	PROBATION	LANKY	PLEADING
PROFOUND	FLOUNCED	FREE SPACE	SLIGHT	MINOR
VAGUE	INTENT	COMMUNE	SOLE	FORMALITIES
HOSTILITY	CONTORTED	SARCASTICALLY	WITTICISM	TACTFULLY

That Was Then, This Is Now Vocabulary

VAGUE	IRRATIONALLY	COMMUNE	RELAPSE	TACTFULLY
MINOR	AFOREMENTIONED	REMINISCING	WITTICISM	ASSAULT
HOSTILITY	INTENT	FREE SPACE	GRAVELY	VENGEFUL
SAUNTERED	HUB	PLEADING	SARCASTICALLY	DESPERATELY
LANKY	ABRUPTLY	HYSTERICAL	INCREDULOUS	FLOUNCED

That Was Then, This Is Now Vocabulary

OBLIGINGLY	INCLINED	SMIRKING	TAUNTING	SOLE
FORMALITIES	LAME	PROBATION	CONTORTED	PROFOUND
SINISTER	SASSY	FREE SPACE	OBSCURE	SLACKED
FLOUNCED	INCREDULOUS	HYSTERICAL	ABRUPTLY	LANKY
DESPERATELY	SARCASTICALLY	PLEADING	HUB	SAUNTERED

That Was Then, This Is Now Vocabulary

REMINISCING	OBSCURE	PLEADING	INCLINED	FLOUNCED
FORMALITIES	ABRUPTLY	WITTICISM	HOSTILITY	ASSAULT
SLACKED	PROFOUND	FREE SPACE	MINOR	RELAPSE
CONTORTED	HYSTERICAL	VAGUE	SASSY	COMMUNE
INCREDULOUS	AFOREMENTIONED	PROBATION	HUB	SLIGHT

That Was Then, This Is Now Vocabulary

GULF	SMIRKING	SAUNTERED	SINISTER	TACTFULLY
TAUNTING	GRAVELY	LANKY	VENGEFUL	INTENT
SARCASTICALLY	DESPERATELY	FREE SPACE	OBLIGINGLY	IRRATIONALLY
SLIGHT	HUB	PROBATION	AFOREMENTIONED	INCREDULOUS
COMMUNE	SASSY	VAGUE	HYSTERICAL	CONTORTED

That Was Then, This Is Now Vocabulary

HYSTERICAL	SARCASTICALLY	MINOR	LAME	AFOREMENTIONED
RELAPSE	SMIRKING	GULF	PLEADING	FLOUNCED
WITTICISM	VENGEFUL	FREE SPACE	HOSTILITY	IRRATIONALLY
SLACKED	ASSAULT	TACTFULLY	INCLINED	PROFOUND
COMMUNE	PROBATION	FORMALITIES	HUB	CONTORTED

That Was Then, This Is Now Vocabulary

ABRUPTLY	REMINISCING	INTENT	OBLIGINGLY	SINISTER
GRAVELY	SASSY	LANKY	DESPERATELY	INCREDULOUS
OBSCURE	TAUNTING	FREE SPACE	SAUNTERED	SLIGHT
CONTORTED	HUB	FORMALITIES	PROBATION	COMMUNE
PROFOUND	INCLINED	TACTFULLY	ASSAULT	SLACKED

That Was Then, This Is Now Vocabulary

INCREDULOUS	HOSTILITY	MINOR	LAME	VENGEFUL
FLOUNCED	ASSAULT	SINISTER	PROFOUND	VAGUE
SASSY	IRRATIONALLY	FREE SPACE	OBSCURE	COMMUNE
GRAVELY	WITTICISM	PLEADING	INTENT	CONTORTED
SARCASTICALLY	TACTFULLY	GULF	HYSTERICAL	SOLE

That Was Then, This Is Now Vocabulary

TAUNTING	SMIRKING	RELAPSE	REMINISCING	HUB
SAUNTERED	ABRUPTLY	FORMALITIES	DESPERATELY	AFOREMENTIONED
LANKY	OBLIGINGLY	FREE SPACE	SLIGHT	INCLINED
SOLE	HYSTERICAL	GULF	TACTFULLY	SARCASTICALLY
CONTORTED	INTENT	PLEADING	WITTICISM	GRAVELY

That Was Then, This Is Now Vocabulary

LAME	ASSAULT	FORMALITIES	RELAPSE	FLOUNCED
VAGUE	SOLE	PLEADING	PROBATION	REMINISCING
SLIGHT	GRAVELY	FREE SPACE	GULF	HYSTERICAL
AFOREMENTIONED	SAUNTERED	SINISTER	HOSTILITY	TAUNTING
OBSCURE	WITTICISM	DESPERATELY	IRRATIONALLY	LANKY

That Was Then, This Is Now Vocabulary

SLACKED	SMIRKING	SARCASTICALLY	ABRUPTLY	TACTFULLY
INTENT	MINOR	VENGEFUL	INCREDULOUS	OBLIGINGLY
COMMUNE	PROFOUND	FREE SPACE	CONTORTED	INCLINED
LANKY	IRRATIONALLY	DESPERATELY	WITTICISM	OBSCURE
TAUNTING	HOSTILITY	SINISTER	SAUNTERED	AFOREMENTIONED

That Was Then, This Is Now Vocabulary

GULF	OBSCURE	IRRATIONALLY	INTENT	INCLINED
SINISTER	AFOREMENTIONED	RELAPSE	COMMUNE	VENGEFUL
PLEADING	PROFOUND	FREE SPACE	HOSTILITY	SMIRKING
VAGUE	DESPERATELY	LAME	INCREDULOUS	FLOUNCED
GRAVELY	OBLIGINGLY	PROBATION	SARCASTICALLY	WITTICISM

That Was Then, This Is Now Vocabulary

SOLE	LANKY	TAUNTING	SLACKED	REMINISCING
HUB	ABRUPTLY	FORMALITIES	SASSY	SLIGHT
CONTORTED	SAUNTERED	FREE SPACE	ASSAULT	HYSTERICAL
WITTICISM	SARCASTICALLY	PROBATION	OBLIGINGLY	GRAVELY
FLOUNCED	INCREDULOUS	LAME	DESPERATELY	VAGUE

That Was Then, This Is Now Vocabulary

SOLE	OBLIGINGLY	ABRUPTLY	DESPERATELY	PROFOUND
AFOREMENTIONED	INCLINED	FORMALITIES	CONTORTED	HUB
ASSAULT	GRAVELY	FREE SPACE	PLEADING	TACTFULLY
REMINISCING	VENGEFUL	SAUNTERED	SLIGHT	FLOUNCED
GULF	INCREDULOUS	SLACKED	LANKY	MINOR

That Was Then, This Is Now Vocabulary

RELAPSE	VAGUE	HYSTERICAL	WITTICISM	COMMUNE
SARCASTICALLY	LAME	PROBATION	TAUNTING	SASSY
INTENT	OBSCURE	FREE SPACE	SINISTER	HOSTILITY
MINOR	LANKY	SLACKED	INCREDULOUS	GULF
FLOUNCED	SLIGHT	SAUNTERED	VENGEFUL	REMINISCING

That Was Then, This Is Now Vocabulary

ASSAULT	AFOREMENTIONED	GRAVELY	IRRATIONALLY	MINOR
SLACKED	OBLIGINGLY	HYSTERICAL	HOSTILITY	TACTFULLY
SOLE	FLOUNCED	FREE SPACE	TAUNTING	SLIGHT
HUB	CONTORTED	PROFOUND	VENGEFUL	SMIRKING
REMINISCING	SINISTER	SASSY	PROBATION	COMMUNE

That Was Then, This Is Now Vocabulary

INCLINED	INCREDULOUS	VAGUE	OBSCURE	ABRUPTLY
SARCASTICALLY	LANKY	LAME	FORMALITIES	INTENT
RELAPSE	SAUNTERED	FREE SPACE	GULF	PLEADING
COMMUNE	PROBATION	SASSY	SINISTER	REMINISCING
SMIRKING	VENGEFUL	PROFOUND	CONTORTED	HUB

That Was Then, This Is Now Vocabulary

HOSTILITY	PROFOUND	FLOUNCED	HYSTERICAL	OBSCURE
PROBATION	CONTORTED	IRRATIONALLY	LAME	OBLIGINGLY
INCREDULOUS	DESPERATELY	FREE SPACE	SINISTER	SOLE
INTENT	VENGEFUL	SASSY	HUB	REMINISCING
VAGUE	ASSAULT	GRAVELY	TACTFULLY	AFOREMENTIONED

That Was Then, This Is Now Vocabulary

INCLINED	FORMALITIES	GULF	WITTICISM	COMMUNE
SMIRKING	SARCASTICALLY	SLACKED	MINOR	RELAPSE
PLEADING	TAUNTING	FREE SPACE	SLIGHT	ABRUPTLY
AFOREMENTIONED	TACTFULLY	GRAVELY	ASSAULT	VAGUE
REMINISCING	HUB	SASSY	VENGEFUL	INTENT

That Was Then, This Is Now Vocabulary

HUB	LANKY	SLIGHT	SARCASTICALLY	SLACKED
TAUNTING	AFOREMENTIONED	SINISTER	ABRUPTLY	ASSAULT
HOSTILITY	VAGUE	FREE SPACE	IRRATIONALLY	PROFOUND
HYSTERICAL	OBLIGINGLY	SAUNTERED	DESPERATELY	SOLE
INCLINED	VENGEFUL	OBSCURE	FORMALITIES	SMIRKING

That Was Then, This Is Now Vocabulary

WITTICISM	PROBATION	GULF	PLEADING	CONTORTED
INTENT	LAME	SASSY	MINOR	GRAVELY
COMMUNE	INCREDULOUS	FREE SPACE	RELAPSE	FLOUNCED
SMIRKING	FORMALITIES	OBSCURE	VENGEFUL	INCLINED
SOLE	DESPERATELY	SAUNTERED	OBLIGINGLY	HYSTERICAL

That Was Then, This Is Now Vocabulary

SASSY	HYSTERICAL	INCREDULOUS	TAUNTING	IRRATIONALLY
GULF	INTENT	SLACKED	LANKY	LAME
GRAVELY	REMINISCING	FREE SPACE	VENGEFUL	SARCASTICALLY
CONTORTED	COMMUNE	PROFOUND	FORMALITIES	WITTICISM
TACTFULLY	RELAPSE	MINOR	SAUNTERED	HUB

That Was Then, This Is Now Vocabulary

SINISTER	SMIRKING	FLOUNCED	ASSAULT	OBSCURE
SOLE	OBLIGINGLY	PROBATION	AFOREMENTIONED	ABRUPTLY
SLIGHT	DESPERATELY	FREE SPACE	INCLINED	HOSTILITY
HUB	SAUNTERED	MINOR	RELAPSE	TACTFULLY
WITTICISM	FORMALITIES	PROFOUND	COMMUNE	CONTORTED

That Was Then, This Is Now Vocabulary

SAUNTERED	ABRUPTLY	SLACKED	GULF	INCLINED
SARCASTICALLY	TACTFULLY	COMMUNE	REMINISCING	GRAVELY
ASSAULT	CONTORTED	FREE SPACE	LAME	SASSY
HUB	SINISTER	VAGUE	AFOREMENTIONED	IRRATIONALLY
TAUNTING	RELAPSE	OBSCURE	HYSTERICAL	PROBATION

That Was Then, This Is Now Vocabulary

VENGEFUL	SLIGHT	FORMALITIES	LANKY	INTENT
MINOR	PROFOUND	INCREDULOUS	PLEADING	OBLIGINGLY
WITTICISM	SMIRKING	FREE SPACE	FLOUNCED	DESPERATELY
PROBATION	HYSTERICAL	OBSCURE	RELAPSE	TAUNTING
IRRATIONALLY	AFOREMENTIONED	VAGUE	SINISTER	HUB

www.ingramcontent.com/pod-product-compliance
Lightning Source LLC
Chambersburg PA
CBHW081457070526
44586CB00019B/2397